Isabella Longobardi

Workforce Planning and Scheduling

Automated Staff Shifts Management and Rostering

GogLiB *ebooks*

ISBN: 9788897527305
First Edition: March 2015

Indice

Foreword

Foreword

The planning of work shifts

The planning of work shifts in all organizations where there are tasks that take place on holidays, during the night or in a continuous cycle is a complex decision-making problem.

In continuous cycle activities, there are tasks that must be guaranteed every day of the week and / or on a 24-hour basis , and therefore it is necessary to assign the shifts required by the service to available operators, while respecting the constraints laid down by national legislation (like the National Labor Relations Act in the U.S.), national labour collective agreements and by company agreements.

The presence of numerous social and professional constraints is often ignored because of the complexity of the decision-making process. And this, in addition to producing an excessive and expensive usage of overtime, can also cause the decision maker to not be aware of violations of laws and contracts, thus exposing the employer to the risk of civil or criminal penalties.

In order to work effectively, anyone who has the task of planning the activities of an organization must learn to perform two tasks that are interconnected but distinct:

- First, he must learn to represent the data specific to his organization's problem in an organized manner, ideally resolving the matter manually, with pen and paper;

- Then, he must learn to use software dedicated to the problem of shift scheduling.

These two dimensions are distinct: it is useless to rush to use a software program before you have planned your organizational problem on paper , and thus before you have answered a series of typical questions:

- At what specific times do people work in my organization?

- In how many different places, or departments, do people work?

- How many different skills or qualifications are needed?

- Which and how many people are available?

- Under which contract conditions do people work?

- Which tasks, or qualifications, can people complete and provide, and in which departments?

This book teaches how to deal with the problem of allocating tasks systematically, and also teaches how to use a dedicated software program to achieve this purpose without wasting time with repetitive tasks in search of the best organizational solution, operations that can be performed by a computer.

The goal is to achieve the ability to quickly and efficiently formulate different solutions that respect the constraints of laws and contracts, to then qualitatively evaluate them and choose the most satisfying one.

Thus, in this book we will first discuss the data analysis of the problem that needs to be addressed before making use of any software tool. We will then proceed by giving examples and referring to one of the most efficient and cheap software solutions available on the market: ZonaTEAM, produced by Zonabit Sistemi.

ZonaTEAM: a software for beginners and experts

ZonaTEAM®, produced by Zonabit Sistemi Srl, is a very convenient software package for both the expert who wants to further improve his management of shifts, and the beginner who wants to become a specialist in the field of organization.

ZonaTEAM is a free download from *http://www.zonabit.it* and is structured to suit beginners: it is fully documented, and has a virtual assistant window that, when started from scratch, shows a step by step process of what fields must be filled to create an initial configuration of the planning.

Setting up a new configuration from scratch using ZonaTEAM looks like this:

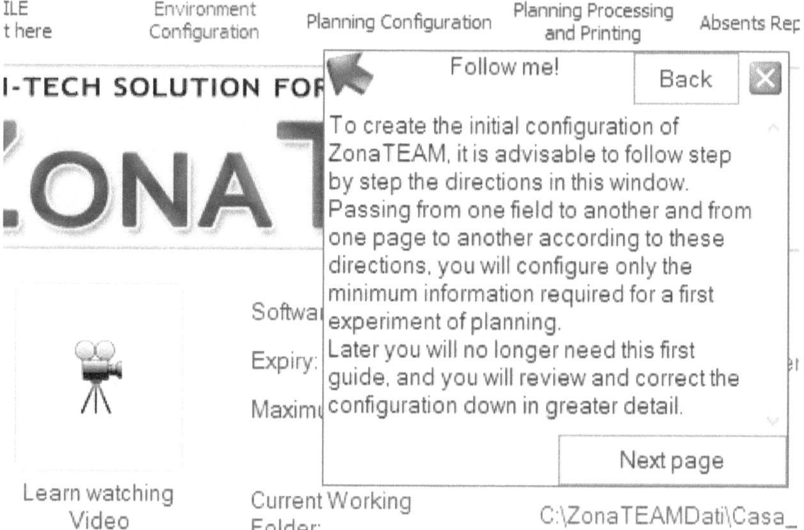

ZonaTEAM provides effective learning tools (very useful, especially instructional videos) and allows you to set up and develop small configurations without the need for any license. At the time that this book is released, you can try the ZonaTEAM software for free with a staff of up to five people. If you wish to set up ZonaTEAM with a more extensive staff, you can buy a license online for a month or a year, at the most affordable market prices.

ZonaTEAM is produced by Zonabit Sistemi Srl, Rome, Italy, and uses proprietary technology for the automatic assignment of shifts, which has proved to be extremely efficient in all scheduling that has been programmed by consulting the authors of this book.

Foreword

1. Description of the problem

In general, the problem faced by those who organize work shifts is that of making very important decisions on behalf of the employing company and for the quality of life of operators working on different tasks.

The performance of the operators is regulated by an employment contract with specific clauses, which indicate the maximum daily and weekly working hours, mandatory rests after a certain number of service hours performed, the allocation of leave and sick days, and other conditions relating to remuneration of overtime, or of work on public holidays.

The software that is used for planning must take these restrictions into account, and therefore must always provide an effectively applicable set of assigned shift, that does not violate the constraints of laws and contracts, and safeguards the general interest of the employer while increasing the quality of life of workers as much as possible.

Violations of law and contract rules can cause civil and criminal penalties; but avoiding sanctions is not the only thing at stake: a good organization, which treats staff fairly, equally sharing the less desirable work shifts without creating disparities between workers, leads to an increase in the productivity of said workers.

Good shift planning must give the employee a sense of being treated fairly and not feel abused by the distribution of the workload either by the employer or by colleagues. The employee will thus not accumulate resentment and grievances that could negatively impact his performance. And to achieve this, the use of a computer tool rather than manual planning is strongly advised, since a computer tool not only will accurately measure the hours of work that must be paid as well as the discomfort arising from disadvantaged shifts, but also, unlike manual scheduling taken out by a person, will never make decisions influenced by unconscious likes and dislikes. When faced with the same situation, a software tool will equally distribute work shifts to those available, whereas manual scheduling may lead to unintentional favouritism and allocating shifts in a biased manner.

In most countries, a large body of legislations, which flank the National Collective Labour Contracts, regulates the employment relationship. These contracts, defined by agreements between trade unions, employers and the government, have the task of adapting national standards to specific production areas.

With some restrictions, collective agreements are allowed to change some parameters of the law provisions, identify exceptions or add even more stringent limitations than those set by the law. It is up to the collective agreements to specify the parameters for the rate of remuneration of workers. Some specific aspects of collective agreements, such as salary, can be redefined at the local or regional level. Each company with its employees must then discuss every collective agreement, at the individual level. This latest negotiation, also known as the individual contract, tends to specify points left open by the national labour contract and to introduce other benefits.

The contract may be extended to employees of other institutions who agree to fully accept the provisions in the individual employment contract.

Factors affecting the organization of work

Organizational constraints

In addition to contractual aspects, that is, the rules applied to the employment relationship, the schedule is affected by the organizational needs of the employer.

Types of shifts according to the schedule

In each scheduling process, the activities must take place in specific time slots. If business hours take place in an unique daily shift, and only on weekdays, the problem of planning does not exist: the staff is normally present, and there is nothing else to do than to schedule vacation days. If the work takes place in a continuous cycle, with activities operating on a 24-hour basis, or which also take place on Sundays and public holidays, the problem of planning arises.

For example, an organization that works on a continuous basis may have the following shifts:

- Morning (6:00 to 14:00)
- Afternoon (14:00 to 10:00 p.m.)
- Night (22:00 to 6:00)
- Cleaning morning (6:00 to 8:00)
- Cleaning evening (20:00 to 22:00)

Any planning is based on a multiplicity of types of shift to manage.

Departments

Almost every business is structured into departments. Some operators may operate only in one department. Others may operate either in multiple departments, or even in every department. Still others, and this is the most common situation, must preferably operate in a given department, and can replace absent colleagues in other departments.

Qualifications and professionalism

Similarly, almost every task is subdivided into professional qualifications. Some operators have only one qualification. Others may operate either with more qualifications, or even with all the existing qualifications. Still others, and this is the most common situation, must operate preferably with a given qualification, which corresponds to their main professional skill, and exceptionally can replace absent colleagues with other qualifications.

Contractual restrictions

Working hours

The working hours determine the quantitative performance limits required of the worker, the distribution of working days in the week and the start and end of each working day. In many countries working hours are fixed by law at 40 hours per week. Individual collective agreements may change this limit.

In all contracts the worker is entitled to at least one day of complete rest lasting 24 hours during the week. The working week can be distributed over five or six days. In a five-day workweek, Saturday is considered the rest day, whereas Sunday is considered a holiday. For a six-day workweek, the rest day often, but not always, coincides with Sunday. The working hours and the number of working days in a week determine the duration of a working day.

The precise definition of the distribution of work shifts, together with the start times and end times of work, is decided by the individual employers. In any case, the worker must be guaranteed a rest day of at least 11 consecutive hours between one working day and the next.

Overtime and extra work

The working hours determine a limit that, in case of necessity, can be exceeded.

The number of hours that exceed base hours, but not the limits set by law, are considered additional work. All the hours that exceed the contract limit are defined as overtime. Generally, overtime is paid at a premium. The maximum number of overtime hours that an employee can work is usually around 250 hours per year. Generally it is not possible to work more than 48 hours in a week. In exceptional cases it is possible to exceed this limit, upon notice to the local Labour Authority.

Overtime is measured monthly with consideration of the total number of hours worked on average in the previous six months, minus the hours already paid as overtime during those months. This allows the creation and management of a kind of time bank where overtime is deposited and withdrawn.

The hours deposited in the bank can be used to compensate for possible hours not worked. These bank hours can also be managed in the opposite way, accounting for hours not worked, which will compensate subsequent overtime. Overtime may be compensated by periods of absence from work. If overtime hours are not compensated, they must be paid at a premium.

Part-time workers

In the case of part-time workers, working hours are reduced according to an agreement between the employee and the employer. The distribution of the hours and days can differ from the standard working time. Overtime is paid at a premium until standard work hours are reached; anything over this preset amount is paid as a full-time worker. In the event that the national collective labour agreement introduces the additional work, it is the duty of the collective agreement to define how much of the surplus labour time should be considered as additional work. For all other aspects, a part-time worker is equivalent to a full time one.

Night work

Any shift having at least an hour in the period from 12 am to 6 am is generally defined as a night shift. Every labour agreement may extend this period. Minors, pregnant women and mothers with children under the age of 2 years may not be assigned to night work. No worker can work more than 8 hours of night shifts within a 24-hour period.

Holidays

Every employee is entitled to a period of leave of at least four weeks per year. Of these, at least two must be used during the year, while the remaining are to be used within 18 months. The holidays are agreed upon between the employee and the employer. There may therefore be a limit to the leave time that the employee can take on a continuous basis, and every leave can be requested by the employee or decided by the employer in order to match the general needs of the organization. It is not allowed to pay sums of money in exchange for leave not taken, except in the case of the end of an employment relationship.

Paid permits

Generally the employee is guaranteed a number of permit hours equal to 24 hours per year. This amount grows at the rate of two hours each month worked. At the end of the year, permits not used are compensated with an allowance.

Diseases

If necessary, the national health system can allocate rest days to the employee. In this case, the employee is justified in not reporting to work, but cannot extend the absence beyond the period certified by a doctor. If the employee is on leave, the days of illness are not counted in the amount of leave taken.

Finding the solution

We therefore always have a set of factors that describe a problem to be solved:

- What activities do we carry out, and in what timeframe?
- Under which conditions can we employ the available persons?

Once the data defining the problem is collected, the process of creating a solution begins, by attempting to assign shifts to the staff that are available in a way that respects all the mandatory constraints. At this point, the use of a software tool will save a great deal of time and work, and will produce a better solution than one obtained by manually scheduling, because the software will avoid errors and will distribute the workload in an even manner.

1. Description of the problem

2. *Before you get to work: questions*

If your only experience with Staff Scheduling is manual – using spreadsheets or sticky notes – you'll need to start out by organizing your basic information to prepare for computerization.

The biggest obstacle is mental: becoming logically aware of what was previously performed subconsciously when manually scheduling.

Therefore before beginning, it is important to answer a series of questions, which were previously mentioned, and that will now be examined in more detail in this chapter.

Does my organization function differently during annual holidays?

One must ask oneself: during the holidays (Christmas, Easter, etc.) is planning and scheduling any different when compared to the corresponding ordinary days? That is, for example, if Christmas falls on a Tuesday, the staff involved will be different from that of any other Tuesday? Or there will be no staff involved, because a vacation of the whole organization is scheduled?

If our organization has more or less staff on hand than is usual during the holidays, we will make a list of holidays for the current year and write down related exceptions. Otherwise, the holidays are not a factor to consider.

What are the hours during which my organization functions?

It is important to distinguish all shifts that have distinct beginning and end, for example, "morning", "afternoon", "night", etc., without taking into account the professional qualifications or departments that are involved in these shifts. Only the start and end time of the different shifts in use should be taken into account.

What contractual work conditions are we bound to?

How many schemes of agreement apply to our employees? It may be that there is only one, because all those involved in the planning work under the same conditions, or it may be that there is more than one contract: namely, that certain employees work full-time, others part time, others according to special agreements and rules. For example, in many organizations the partners or owners delegate management responsibilities and take charge of executive tasks only when the staff is insufficient on account of vacation or illness. In this case, there exists a "Partners" contract, which has different rules than the contracts applied to regular employees.

It should be noted that this "Partners" contract is not formally signed, unlike the employee contracts, and yet it is still applied and has the same relevance as the contracts of the regular employees for scheduling.

The types of contracts to be applied must therefore be specified , and for each contract the most important features must be noted:

How many hours of service are there in an ordinary day?

How many maximum hours of service can be assigned in a day (including any overtime or recovery, or times to cover exceptionally long shifts)?

How many hours of service are there in a normal week?

How many hours of maximum service (including any overtime or recovery) are there in the week?

How many total hours of work are to be paid in the calendar year?

For example:

In total, 40 hours X 48 weeks = 1920 hours.

And how many total hours of leave or paid leave?

For example:

Vacation and Leave: 35 days, ordinary hours per day 8, 35 X 8 = 280 hours.

How many overtime hours are allowed per month or per year?

At what times of day is the work considered night work?

Are there special limits for night work?

Answer all these questions keeping in mind the conditions actually applied to employees. If the answers are the same for all employees, it means that there is only one contract. Otherwise, there are more than one.

A detail: normally the difference between employees and shareholders or owners is specified in the contract conditions. Employees, for example, have an absolute limit of 40 or 48 hours a week, while the shareholders who lend themselves to cover absent employees can exceptionally work well over this limit. But employees must provide a given number of work hours per year, about 2000 for full time, while the shareholders must be work as little as possible on executive tasks, even zero hours per year if there are never any unplanned absences.

In how many different places, or departments, do we work?

The departments are the physical locations where people work. Is there one, or more than one? List them all.

How many different skills or qualifications are needed?

Is there only one or more than one professional skill needed in scheduling for the organization ? Even here, list all professional qualifications that are necessary. Caution: If there are activities that do not take place either during the night, on Sundays or during public holidays, they probably will not be a problem for planning. Thus, leave out the qualifications corresponding to these activities.

Which and how many people are available?

List the persons involved in the scheduling, and for each focus specifically on the contract that applies.

What qualifications can define people's work, and in which departments?

For each staff member, one must ask:

In which department can he work? In all, or only in some?

Which professional qualifications can he take out? All, or only some?

Are there departments where the person should be preferably used, and in which departments should he be used only exceptionally, to replace other unavailable employees?

Are there qualifications that the person should preferably take out , and qualifications that should be only used in exceptional cases, to replace other unavailable employees?

The first test scheduling will be done by beginning with any day of the current year. For each person, it is good to note if he started working for the organization since the beginning of the current year, or whether he has been hired more recently. Later on we will see that this information will be useful to correctly allocate the workload.

Are there people with special constraints and preferences?

Are there people to whom special rules apply? For example: people whose shifts must take place in the afternoon, or whose night shifts must be minimized? Or: are there apprentices who cannot perform certain jobs if a senior member does not accompany them?

It is good to have an exact picture of these exceptional conditions.

In what time frame do we want to begin planning?

It is good to start planning a month ahead of time, and to avoid attempting longer term scheduling.

One thing to focus on: In our case, is it better to plan for entire months ahead of time, from the first to the last day, or for 4 or

5 weeks at a time, e.g. from the first Monday of each month to the first Sunday of the following month?

For example, are shifts normally planned from the first of March until March 31, or from Monday, March 2 until Sunday, March 29, or Sunday, April 5?

Which staff is needed?

How many people are needed:

- On the different days of the week?
- In different departments?
- With different professional qualifications?
- During different shifts (morning, afternoon, evening, night)?

For example: how many people are needed on Monday, in the "motherhood", department with the title of "nurse" during the "morning" the shift?

Make a table that includes all the scheduling needs.

Then, ask yourself: in every item that is put in the table, how many employees are necessary, and how many others may eventually be added, if there is time to recover?

Does our scheduling follow different weekly templates?

In most cases there is only one scheduling scheme that applies.

However, there are exceptional situations.

For example, the scheduling of a pharmacy could be based on the alternation between ordinary weeks, in which the shop is only open during the day on weekdays, and special weeks, in which the shop is also open on holidays and nights. It may be convenient to identify coverage templates that will help maintain the information about the necessary staff and the time limits that must be followed in the two types of weeks, then quickly put them in monthly schedules.

Do we already know the foreseen leave periods?

If yes, they will be immediately taken into account.

Otherwise, they will be taken account as the schedule is updated.

Are there people that will be available only at certain times?

If yes, this will have to be taken into account.

Before beginning the set up of your scheduling, make sure to have a good idea of your organization structure, that way you have the answers to these questions ready before your start.

3. Formal Data Analysis

In the previous chapter the sequence of preliminary questions to planning work has helped us to bring out the character of the basic information of a planning. But to effectively manage a schedule we should be able to perform a more formal analysis of the data involved and the relationships among them.

In this chapter we will use the most common notation used in the construction of the logical schema of a relational database: the Entity-Relationship diagram.

An entity is defined as a collection of objects that occur with the same properties, such as: entity Employees XXX = set of people working with a contract for the firm XXX.

Relationship between two entities, instead, means a correspondence between the individual elements of the two entities. For example: we can imagine the relationship "generates" connecting two entities "mothers" and "children": one mother is in relation with one or more children (individual elements of the two entities), a children has only one mother.

For more details on these concepts, see:

http://en.wikipedia.org/wiki/Entity%E2%80%93relationship_m odel

In shifts scheduling we shall begin identifying the entities involved. We will refer to the environment in which shifts will be scheduled with the name Organization.

DEPARTMENTS Entity

The first step is to consider the departments which make up the Organization. You will therefore have the Departments Entity given by all the departments.

It's important to note that departments should actually distinguish the areas of the Organization.

Below are presented examples that clarify the concept.

<u>Organization - Department store.</u>

Departments: man clothes, woman clothes, kids clothes, showcases.

There are three Departments that distinguish the logistics division of a department store and a more generic department for the setting up of the showcases

<u>Organization – Nursing Home</u>

Departments*:* women building, men building, general rooms. As in the previous example, there are 2 departments one for men and one for women and the group of general rooms: canteen, halls etc.

<u>Organization - Manufacturing company.</u>

Departments: carpentry, painting

QUALIFICATIONS Entity

Every person working for the Organization carries out one or more tasks, or qualifies for certain types of work and not for others. The second entity will certainly be given by all the different tasks carried out by the staff, called qualifications.

In this case you should pay close attention to the general concept of qualification that does not correspond to the individual but to groups of people.

Here are some examples to clarify the concept.

<u>Organization - Department store</u>

Departments: man clothes, woman clothes, kids clothes, showcases.

Qualifications: vendor, window dresser, cleaning agent, cashier.

The Qualifications can be used in one or more Departments and do not specify the individual, but the existing tasks.

It would be wrong to introduce into Qualifications: *man clothes vendor, woman clothes vendor*, because if the work is the same, the qualification will be the same and different will be only the department in which it takes place.

<u>Organization – Nursing Home</u>

Departments: women building, men building, general rooms.

Qualifications: nurse, canteen employee, cleaning agent, supervisor.

Again it would be wrong to introduce into Qualifications: *cleaning agent women building*, *cleaning agent men building*, because, if the work is the same, the qualification will be the same and different will be only the department in which it takes place.

<u>Organization - Manufacturing company.</u>

Departments: carpentry, painting

Qualifications: operative, foreman, painter

EMPLOYEES Entity

The third entity to consider is the Employees entity, whose elements are all those who work within the Organization and that must be considered in shifts scheduling.

For each person you will need to gather some mandatory data: Qualifications for which each person is enabled, Qualifications that they can cover only in replacement (when the staff specifically trained is absent), Departments in which he can be work, employment contract (full time, part time, temporary etc.), personal limitations to the performance of his service, preferences etc.

We will return to these issues in more detail later.

SHIFT TYPES Entity

This entity will contain as its elements all different shift types taking place within the Organization.

Each shift type will have the two main attributes: start time and end time; these will allow to calculate the real duration of the shift.

You now need to identify which shift types are really different within your Organization.

In general you can identify them thinking about the time slots to which they refer. For example: morning, afternoon, evening.

If a type of shift is carried out in different Departments or different Qualifications but has always the same slot of time it must be specified only once.

See below an example.

<u>Organization - Department store.</u>

Departments: man clothes, woman clothes, kids clothes, showcases.

Qualifications: vendor, window dresser, cleaning agent, cashier.

Shift types: morning (9-14) afternoon (14-20) cleaning (7-9)

There are only three kind of shifts because in this Organization time slots are the same for vendors, window dressers and for the cashier. The cleaning agents instead have a different shift schedule and therefore they have their own shift type.

<u>Organization – Nursing Home</u>

Departments: women building, men building, general rooms.

Qualifications: nurse, canteen employee, cleaning agent, supervisor.

Shift types: morning (7-14) afternoon (14-21) night (21-7) cleaning (12-19) lunch time (11-15) dinner time (17-21)

There are six kinds of shifts.

In this example the assumption is that time slots are the same whether working in women department or in men department, whether people perform the job of supervisor or of nurse.

But the cleaning agents and the attendants at the canteen have different working hours, so for them you need to create new types of shifts.

<u>Organization - Manufacturing company.</u>

Departments: carpentry, painting

Qualifications: operative, foreman, painter

Shift types*:* morning (7-14) afternoon (14-21) night (21-7)

In the specification of the various shift types you shall take into account many other elements that concur to identify the peculiar characteristics of your Organization.

Almost no actually existing organization is so simple. Often there are many more shift types: from those which provide a lunch break, to those that provide a break after a specific number of hours of work and so on.

All of these features, however, refer to the employment contract and will be analyzed in the chapter devoted to the contracts.

CONTRACTS Entity

In the simplest organizations this entity will contain a single element: the single contract that is applied to every employee.

But in most cases the employee have different contracts; just think only of full-time and part-time contracts.

For each specific contract you must create an element of the entity Contracts.

The contractual conditions applied in planning are the attributes of this entity.

They are many: the number of hours of work per day and per week, the number of holiday and vacations, the number of weekly rest periods, overtime hours allowed etc.

Listed below are the attributes useful for planning.

Hours of ordinary service in a day

Number of hours of work to do in a day. When engaging in a day exceeds this value, the excess hours are considered overtime, or recovery of previous permits / Vacation / Absences.

Maximum hours of service in a day

Hours of service maximum that can be assigned in a day (including any Overtime or recovery).

Minimum break between two shifts

Hours of minimum break between Shifts. This data is highly significant for plannings involving alternating morning, afternoon and night Shifts.

For example, if the minimum break is 11 Hours, and if a Person has paid service between 6:00 and 14:00, he cannot be engaged in the subsequent night Shift that begins at 22:00 (i.e., after only 8 Hours).

Hours of ordinary service in a week.

Number of hours of work to do in a week.

Maximum hours of service in a week

Hours of service maximum that can be assigned in a week (including any Overtime or recovery).

NOTE: The week is normally seven days, but some plannings may have limits similar to weekly ones over a shorter period (for example, the standard service could be 30 Hours every six days).

Hours of rest

Hours of rest without assigned commitments, mandatory weekly, therefore normally after 5 or 6 days on duty.

NOTE: The week is normally 7 days, but some tiresome activities may require a closer constraint, such as 24 Hours of rest every 6 or 5 days, therefore after 5 or 4 days on duty.

Additional hourly limit

If necessary a second limit, in addition to the weekly one, can be established. For example, there are schedules in which there is the limit of 40 hours weekly every 7 days, and also an additional limit of 72 hours every fourteen days, because by the contract the weeks have alternately 5 and 4 working days.

There is also the case where the second limit applies only if the employee has work commitments on Saturday and/or Sunday.

Meal break

he lunch break allows the interruption of the activity of a working day without applying the minimum break required between Shifts.

For example, if a business provides morning or afternoon Shifts, lunch breaks can be set between 12:00 and 16:00.

If an activity involves continuous Shifts of 7 or 8 Hours, lunch break is not to be set up (after each Shift the requirement of minimum break must be met).

Duties in replacement

The Replacement engagements are those in which a Person is assigned to a Qualifications that is lower of his professional degree, in order to substitute other not available Persons (because absent, or already used to the maximum Contract Hours). Since the Shifts in Substitution should be kept to a minimum, you should always set a cost higher than 1.00 for the Substitutions. Usually assign the cost 1.50 to Substitutions and 2.00 to Overtime. Later, you can adjust this value in order to use Overtime or Substitution in the optimal proportion.

Overtime

Overtime Hours maximum payable in the month and year. The Overtime paid beyond those limits is not permitted. Those within these limits are allowed, but the calculation of Planning will reduce the use to a minimum, and if possible will avoid overtime at all..

Nocturnal work

A shift is considered Nocturnal if it is wholly or partly within the limits set up here.

CAUTION: for example, if there were only Shifts 06:00-14:00, 14:00-22:00, 22:00-6:00, the limits on night work would obviously be 22:00 to 6:00. But if there was also an evening Shift 15:00-23:00, and this should not be considered nocturnal, then the night the interval should be set up as 23:00-6:00. Shifts 22:00 to 6:00 would be considered nocturnal, because they are within this range (even if only PARTIALLY).

Maximum night shift length

This data is useful in cases where there are several types of night Shift, short, which could be allocated following one another for the same Person (e.g. from 22:00 to 01:00 a task, from 1:00 to 4:00 another task, etc.).

Maximum number of consecutive night Shifts

After which a rest must be given.

Break after consecutive shifts minimum

Hours of rest required after a series of night Shifts.

Weekend

Weekend time limits. This data is required to distribute approximately the Weekend commitments in the most equitable way.

Maximum consecutive weekends

The constraint of Maximum consecutive Weekends with commitments is mandatory and is respected exactly.

Relationship between DEPARTMENTS and QUALIFICATIONS

In any organization there is a close relationship between Departments and Qualifications. In every department, in fact, it is possible that only some qualifications are requested.

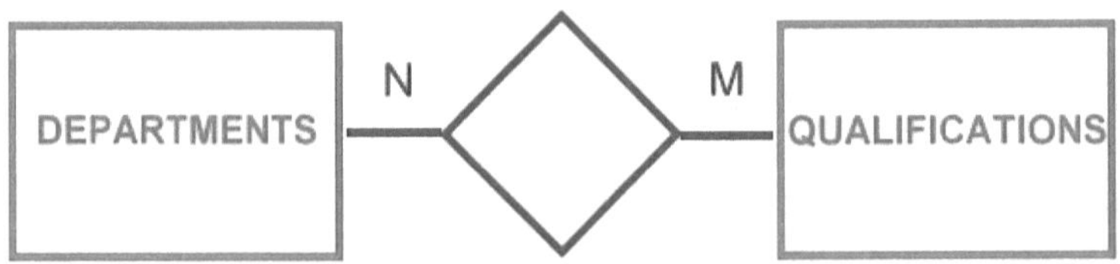

It's helpful to look at the examples.

<u>Organization - Department store.</u>

Departments: man clothes, woman clothes, kids clothes, showcases.

Qualifications: vendor, window dresser, cleaning agent, cashier.

Shift types: morning (9-14) afternoon (14-20) cleaning (7-9)

Employee: Catherine (vendor) John (cleaning agent) Mary (window dresser) Edward (cashier) Jennifer (vendor) and so on.

Relationship Departments-Qualifications:

vendor-man clothes,

vendor-woman clothes,

vendor-kids clothes,

cashier-man clothes,

cashier-woman clothes,

cleaning agent-man clothes,

cleaning agent-woman clothes,

cleaning agent-kids clothes

window dresser-showcases

<u>Organization – Nursing Home</u>

Departments: women building, men building, general rooms.

Qualifications: nurse, canteen employee, cleaning agent, supervisor.

Shift types: morning (7-14) afternoon (14-21) night (21-7) cleaning (12-19) lunch time (11-15) dinner time (17-21)

Employee: Catherine (nurse) John (cleaning agent) Mary (supervisor) Edward (canteen employee) Jennifer (nurse) Henry (supervisor) Rebecca (cleaning agent) and so on.

Relationship Departments-Qualifications:

women building-nurse

men building-nurse

women building-supervisor

men building-supervisor

general rooms-supervisor

general rooms-canteen employee

women building-cleaning agent

men building-cleaning agent

general rooms-cleaning agent

<u>Organization - Manufacturing company.</u>

Departments: carpentry, painting

Qualifications: operative, foreman, painter

Shift types: morning (7-14) afternoon (14-21) night (21-7)

Relationship Departments-Qualifications:

operative-carpentry,

painter-painting,

foreman-carpentry,

foreman-painting

You will notice that the qualification operative is allowed only in the carpentry department, as well as the qualification painter is allowed only in the painting department, while the foreman qualification is permitted in both Departments.

Relationship between *QUALIFICATIONS* and *EMPLOYEES*

Each person working within an organization has a specific qualification and performs a specific task.

But sometimes an employee can perform different tasks (specified by different Qualifications) either as ordinary or in replacement of qualified employees.

As we see from the ER diagram to the relationship between Employee and Qualification belong some attributes necessary to specify in detail the conditions under which the employee carries that given activity.

The attributes are:

department and mode.

It's possible that the person performs a specific task only at a department and with a certain qualification and another with the same qualification in another department, or who performs the same task in all Departments with the same qualification and so on.

To each pair department-qualification is associated a mode: ordinary job, replacement, replacement in exceptional cases etc.

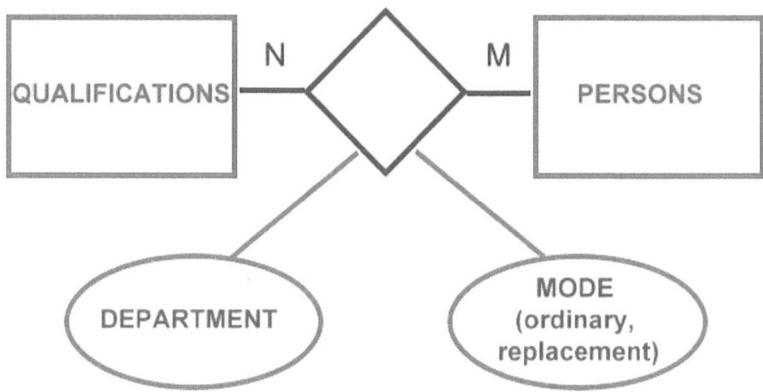

Here are some examples.

<u>Organization - Department store.</u>

Departments: man clothes, woman clothes, kids clothes, showcases.

Qualifications: vendor, window dresser, cleaning agent, cashier.

Shift types : morning (9-14) afternoon (14-20) cleaning (7-9)

Employee: Catherine (vendor) John (cleaning agent) Mary (window dresser) Edward (cashier) Jennifer (vendor) an so on.

Relationship between Departments and Qualifications:

vendor-man clothes,

vendor-woman clothes,

vendor-kids clothes,

cashier-man clothes,

cashier-woman clothes,

cleaning agent-man clothes,

cleaning agent-woman clothes,

cleaning agent-kids clothes

window dresser-showcases

Relationship between Qualifications and Employees:

Catherine-woman clothes-vendor- ordinary task

Catherine-woman clothes-cashier- replacement

Mary-showcases-window dresser- ordinary task

Edward-man clothes-cashier- ordinary task

Edward-woman clothes-cashier- ordinary task

Edward-man clothes-vendor- replacement

and so on.

<u>Organization – Nursing Home</u>

Departments: women building, men building, general rooms.

Qualifications: nurse, canteen employee, cleaning agent, supervisor.

Shift types: morning (7-14) afternoon (14-21) night (21-7) cleaning (12-19) lunch time (11-15) dinner time (17-21)

Employee: Catherine (nurse) John (cleaning agent) Mary (supervisor) Edward (canteen employee) Jennifer (nurse) Henry (supervisor) Rebecca (cleaning agent) and so on.

Relationship between Departments and Qualifications:

women building-nurse

men building-nurse

women building-supervisor

men building-supervisor

general rooms-supervisor

general rooms-canteen employee

women building-cleaning agent

men building-cleaning agent

general rooms-cleaning agent

Relationship between Qualifications and Employees:

Catherine-nurse-women building- ordinary task

Jennifer-women building clothes-nurse- ordinary task

Jennifer-men building clothes-nurse- replacement

Rebecca-men building clothes-cleaning agent- ordinary task

Rebecca-women building clothes-cleaning agent- ordinary task

and so on.

Organization - Manufacturing company.

Departments: carpentry, painting

Qualifications: operative, foreman, painter

Shift types: morning (7-14) afternoon (14-21) night (21-7)

Employee: Catherine (painter) John (foreman) Mary (operative/painter) Edward (operative) Jennifer (foreman) Henry (operative) Rebecca (foreman) and so on.

Relationship between Departments and Qualifications:

operative-carpentry,

painter-painting,

foreman-carpentry,

foreman-painting

Relationship between Qualifications and Employees:

Catherine-painting-painter-- ordinary task

John-carpentry-foreman- ordinary task

John- painting-foreman- ordinary task

Jennifer-carpentry-foreman- replacement

Jennifer- painting-foreman- ordinary task

Edward-carpentry-operative- ordinary task

and so on.

Relationship between CONTRACTS and EMPLOYEES

The relationship between the contracts and the employees is a 1:N relationship, where every person has one contract and the same contract corresponds to more employees.

If the specific contract of a person has additional conditions that this person has agreed with the Organization, it is recommended to create a special contract to be used only for that person or for those who have the same contractual conditions.

Do not confuse the contract terms with the limitations and personal preferences.

These are attributes of the relationship between Contracts and Employee and do not constitute a different contract.

For example, if the employees Anna and Mary have a normal fulltime contract, but Mary cannot work on Monday morning, the contract is the same but it will be necessary to specify in the personal limitations of Mary the inability to work on Monday morning.

You can see below the possible personal limitations. and preferences.

<u>Personal preferences</u>

Pay attention to specify the preferences that you can meet, because preferences are binding for planning purposes.

A very common case is that in which the Employee prefers not to work on Saturday afternoon or Sunday: If the maximum availability declared in the preferences isn't enough, the shifts can't be filled.

NOTE: It is necessary to distinguish between requirements directly expressed by the Employee, and requirements that should favor the satisfaction of certain requirements by OTHER Employee. For example: Jones wants to work on Saturday just once a month, while Smith is willing to work on Saturday without difficulty. Configure that Jones can only work 8 Hours on 160 on Saturday, then not more than 5%, and do NOT configure ANYTHING for Smith, which obviously will be used on Saturday in place of Jones.

Preferred time brackets

An employee can express the preference for certain types of Shifts or time brackets. For example, to be engaged in the morning to up to 25% of his work time, or being engaged in the evening at least 30%, and so on.

Limits on specified shifts

This data are useful to fairly distribute the tasks that the staff usually likes less.

Use these values to establish limitations to the shifts in a given [department] and/or [qualification] and/or [shift type]. Each data is optional, but at least one should be specified.

There other conditions too:

the minimum or maximum of consecutive days in which you can assign the person to the given department/qualification/shift type, and/or the maximum of shifts in the given department/qualification/shift type which can be given in a period of n days, calculated on the base of the average in the planning period, and/or

the pause in days that must be observed before coming back to the given department/qualification/shift type.

Consecutive shifts

There are organizations where certain employees must be committed with a constant alternating rhythm, for example: 2 days in the morning, 2 in the afternoon.

Or for the case where a certain type of shift should be grouped in sequences (e.g., the shift "Kitchen" must be assigned in sequences long from 3 to 5 days).

 Personal limitations

Tutor

Sometimes Tutor is mandatory. This obligation must be considered only in the case that a person can be engaged with a given qualification in a given department only under the condition that another person, enabled to the qualification configured for the tutor, is present in the department.

This configuration is useful if there are apprentices or young employees that cannot have the responsibility of a given qualification, and need to be monitored by an older or more qualified staff member.

Presence forbidden in given time brackets and days

n addition to the constraints specified above, there are cases in which a person cannot be committed:

in a given department, or

with a given qualification, or

in a given department and with a given qualification

in the specified time bracket and/or in the specified days of the weeks (and/or holydays).

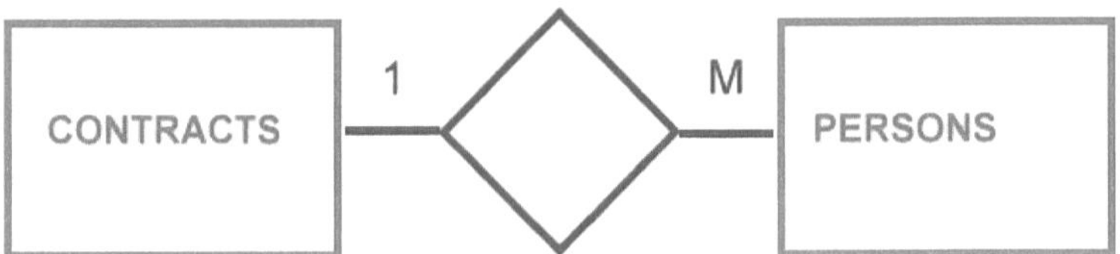

Examples:

<u>Organization - Department store.</u>

In this organization all employees are hired either full time or part time, so that they all follow the same rules, regardless of their qualification. Only the cleaners have a separate contract, because their work load and working time is different than all the others.

Contracts: full time, part time, cleaning agents

Employee: Catherine (vendor) John (cleaning agent) Mary (window dresser) Edward (cashier) Jennifer (vendor) and so on.

Relationship between Contracts and Employee:

Catherine-full time

John-cleaning agents

Mary-part time

Edward-full time

and so on.

<u>Organization – Nursing Home</u>

In this organization nurses and canteen employees are all employed full time by following the same rules, regardless of their qualification. The cleaners and supervisors instead have a separate contract, because the work load and working time is special for their task.

Contracts: full time, cleaning agents, supervisors.

Employee: Catherine (nurse) John (cleaning agent) Mary (supervisor) Edward (canteen employee) Jennifer (nurse) Henry (supervisor) Rebecca (cleaning agent) and so on.

Relationship between Contracts and Employees:

Catherine-full time

Jennifer-full time

Rebecca-cleaning agents

Henry-supervisors

and so on.

<u>Organization - Manufacturing company.</u>

In this company the owners perform the task of foreman only when there are not enough employees available to fill this task. So the owners have a contract with rules aside: is not a formally signed contract, but it's applied in the planning. All other employees are employed on full or part time, with the same rules regardless of their qualification.

Contracts: owners, full time, part time

Shift types: morning (7-14) afternoon (14-21) night (21-7)

Employee: Catherine (painter) John (foreman) Mary (operative/painter) Edward (operative) Jennifer (foreman)

Henry (operative) Paul (foreman) Rebecca (foreman) and so on.

Relationship between Contracts and Employees:

Catherine-full time

John-owners

Jennifer-full time

Edward-part time

Henry-part time

Paul-owners

Rebecca-part time

and so on.

Relationship between QUALIFICATIONS and SHIFT TYPES

The relationship between the Qualifications and Shift types must be analyzed very carefully because it produces the coverage of shifts in all the schedules that will be processed.

This relationship specifies exactly for each type of shift the real coverage necessity.

As it appears in the ER diagram it has some attributes that allow you to specify the availability of employee required for each pair: qualification-shift type

The main attributes are: department, mandatory number

of employees, optional number of employees, qualification.

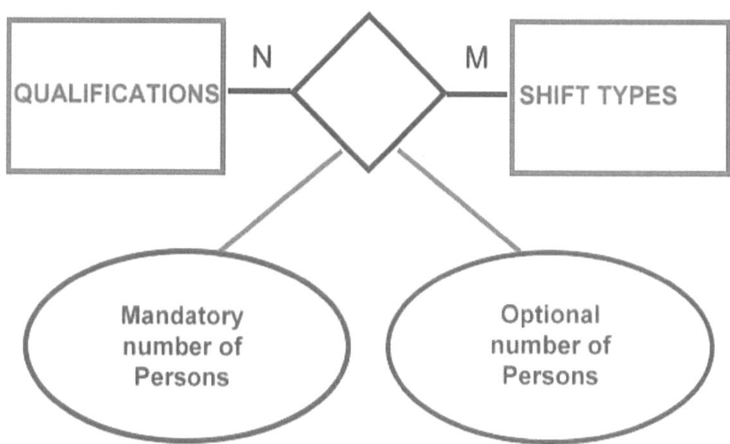

Examples:

<u>Organization - Department store.</u>

Departments: man clothes, woman clothes, kids clothes, showcases.

Qualifications: vendor, window dresser, cleaning agent, cashier.

Shift types : morning (9-14) afternoon (14-20) cleaning (7-9)

Employee: Catherine (vendor) John (cleaning agent) Mary (window dresser) Edward (cashier) Jennifer (vendor) and so on.

Relationship between Departments and Qualifications:

vendor-man clothes,

vendor-woman clothes,

vendor-kids clothes,

cashier-man clothes,

cashier-woman clothes,

cleaning agent-man clothes,

cleaning agent-woman clothes,

cleaning agent-kids clothes

window dresser-showcases

Relationship between Qualifications and Employee:

Catherine-woman clothes-vendor- ordinary task

Catherine-woman clothes-cashier- replacement

Mary-showcases-window dresser- ordinary task

Edward-man clothes-cashier- ordinary task

Edward-woman clothes-cashier- ordinary task

Edward-man clothes-vendor- replacement

and so on.

Relationship between Qualifications-Shift types:

window dresser-morning-showcases-1-0 (one employees is mandatory, no additional employee)

vendor-morning-man clothes-2-1 (two employees are mandatory, one additional employee admitted)

vendor-afternoon-man clothes-3-1

vendor- morning -woman clothes-1-1

vendor- afternoon -woman clothes-2-2

and so on.

Organization – Nursing Home

Departments: women building, men building, general rooms.

Qualifications: nurse, canteen employee, cleaning agent, supervisor.

Shift types: morning (7-14) afternoon (14-21) night (21-7) cleaning (12-19) lunch time (11-15) dinner time (17-21)

Employee: Catherine (nurse) John (cleaning agent) Mary (supervisor) Edward (canteen employee) Jennifer (nurse) Henry (supervisor) Rebecca (cleaning agent) and so on.

Relationship between Departments and Qualifications:

women building-nurse

men building-nurse

women building-supervisor

men building-supervisor

general rooms-supervisor

general rooms-canteen employee

women building-cleaning agent

men building-cleaning agent

general rooms-cleaning agent

Relationship between Qualifications and Employees:

Catherine-nurse-women building- ordinary task

Jennifer-women building clothes-nurse- ordinary task

Jennifer-men building clothes-nurse- replacement

Rebecca-men building clothes-cleaning agent- ordinary task

Rebecca-women building clothes-cleaning agent- ordinary task

and so on.

Relationship between Qualifications-Shift types:

nurse-night-women building-1-0 (one employee is mandatory, no additional employees admitted)

nurse-morning-women building-2-2

nurse- morning -men building-2-1

supervisor- morning -general rooms-4-0

supervisor-afternoon-men building-1-1

and so on.

<u>Organization - Manufacturing company.</u>

Departments: carpentry, painting

Qualifications: operative, foreman, painter

Shift types: morning (7-14) afternoon (14-21) night (21-7)

Employee: Catherine (painter) John (foreman) Mary (operative/painter) Edward (operative) Jennifer (foreman) Henry (operative) Rebecca (foreman) and so on.

Relationship between Departments and Qualifications:

operative-carpentry,

painter-painting,

foreman-carpentry,

foreman-painting

Relationship between Qualifications and Employees:

Catherine-painting-painter- ordinary task

John-carpentry-foreman- ordinary task

John- painting-foreman- ordinary task

Jennifer-carpentry-foreman- replacement

Jennifer- painting-foreman- ordinary task

Edward-carpentry-operative- ordinary task

and so on.

Relationship between Qualifications-Shift types:

foreman-morning-carpentry-1-0

foreman- morning -painting-1-0

foreman-afternoon-carpentry-1-0

foreman- afternoon -painting-1-0

foreman-night-carpentry-1-0

operative- morning -painting-2-1

operative- afternoon -painting-2-1

operative- night -painting-0-1

and so on.

4. Solving the problem with ZonaTEAM

ZonaTEAM is structured corresponding to what has been described until here. ZonaTEAM allows us to configure the organizational and contractual constraints that define our problem, and then is able to search for us an optimal solution.

ZonaTEAM is a free download from ***http://www.zonabit.it*** and is structured to fit beginners. At the time of this book, you can try for free ZonaTEAM with a staff of five people. If you want to set up ZonaTEAM with a more extensive staff, you can buy a license online for a month or a year, at the most affordable prices of the market.

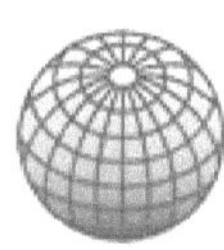

To use ZonaTEAM, you need to build your configuration step by step following the suggested order.

So, you must first setup the environment (contracts of employment, available people), then the planning data (time to plan, staff needed), then set up and print your schedule.

Do not jump from one point to another, but follow the suggested order.

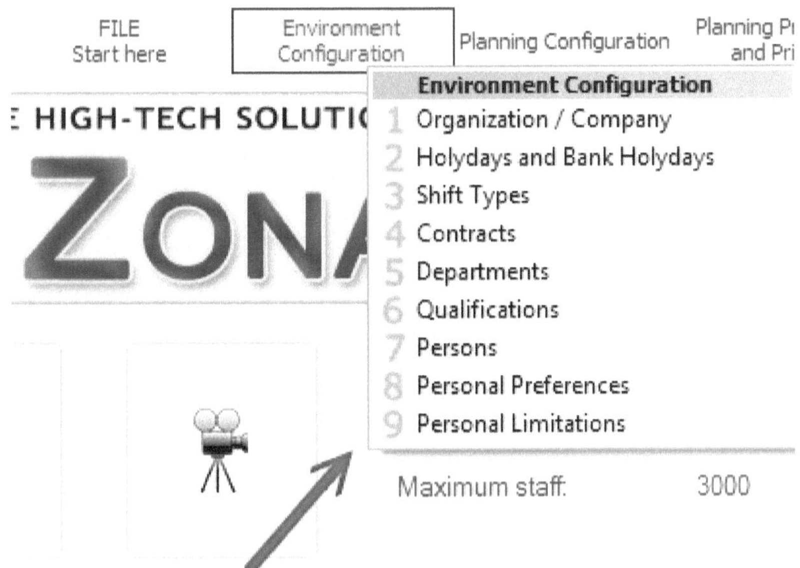

Follow the suggested order!

Now in this chapter we will setup the scheduling of "Smith Carpentry" step by step, an organization that works continuously, with day and night shifts, in two departments, and that allows us to illustrate some common characteristics of many schedules.

It's not realistic to get it perfect the first try. You must first be able to build and process a very simple rough draft, then improve the configuration again until you get a perfect result.

Work environment configuration

As the download of ZonaTEAM is free, the best way to follow the exposition from here on is to install the software, create a test folder and read the book while browsing ZonaTEAM configuration panels.

After creating the folder for planning, go to the environment configuration.

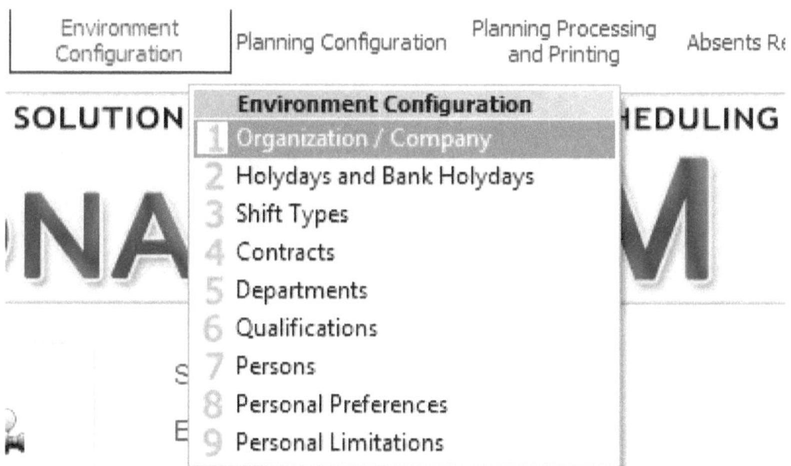

First of all, in the configuration of the environment, we need to specify only the name of the company.

In general, remember to leave the information blank you do not need, or when you have not yet understood the function: you will go back to these fields later, after having completed a preliminary test.

For every configuration field there is a help button, explaining the function of the data to be entered. Refer continually to the help keys.

Holydays and bank holydays

In the second step of the configuration we enter current year holidays.

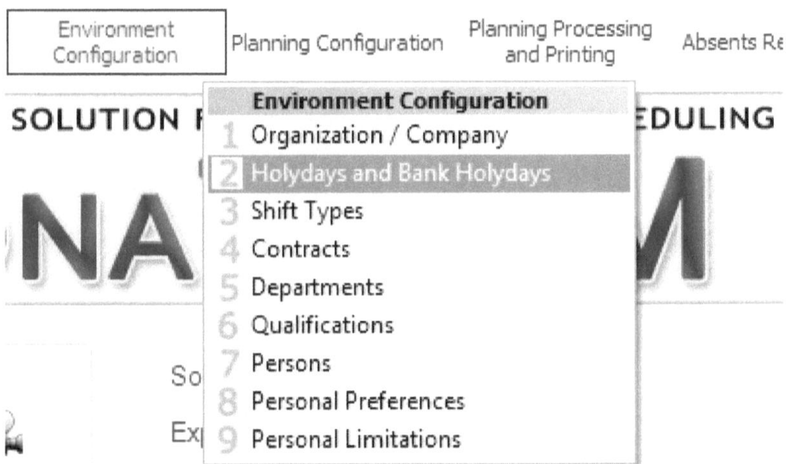

To automatically create the default public holidays there is a dedicated key. In organizations where the staff works Saturday and Sundays, Christmas and Easter with no distinction you can skip this step.

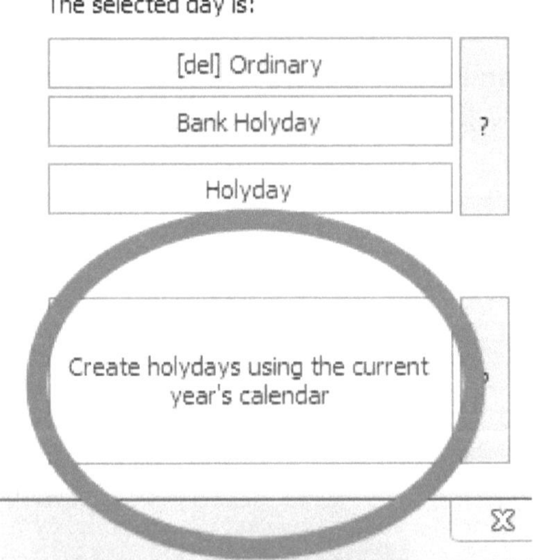

But since Smith Carpentry in our example does not work either Sunday or public holidays, we use the key that creates default calendar public holidays: so the staff will not be engaged, for example, on Christmas.

Shift types

In the next step you enter all the kinds of shifts in use.

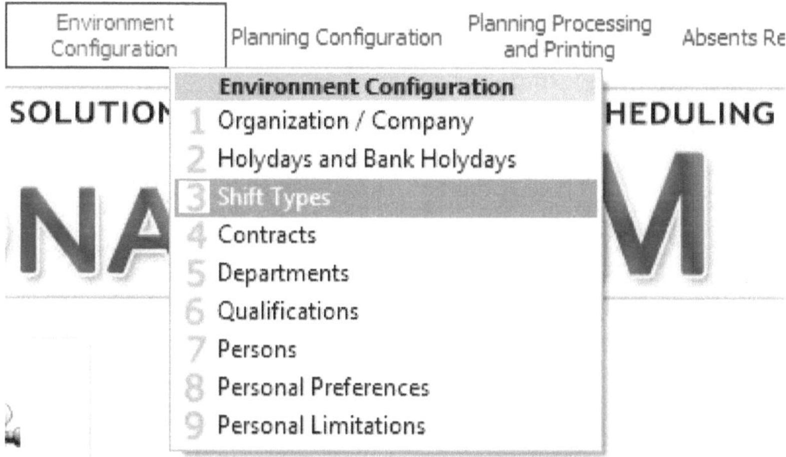

Warning: here the shifts are simply time intervals. You must simply insert the shifts that have distinct beginning and end times, such as morning, afternoon, night and so on, without taking into account the departments or the qualifications that are involved in these shifts.

A frequent error to avoid, is to multiply the shifts for no reason. For example, it would be wrong to set up a shift "morning carpentry " and another " morning painting ", if in fact there is only one shift in the morning, which lasts from 6 a.m. to 2 p.m.

In "Smith Carpentry" we have three eight-hour shifts that cover the entire day, plus a cleaning shift lasting two hours.

Name of shift type	Start Hour	End Hour	Duration Hours	Priority in the equable distribution
<Add>				
Morning	06:00	14:00	8:00	none
Afternoon	14:00	22:00	8:00	none
Cleaning	14:00	16:00	2:00	none
Night	22:00	06:00	8:00	high

You can assign a priority in the equitable distribution to staff to each shift. Here we gave high priority to the night shift, because obviously you have to assign it as evenly as possible among all the staff.

Employment contracts

In the next step, the contracts, we must insert the employment contracts, which are the most complex data to configure.

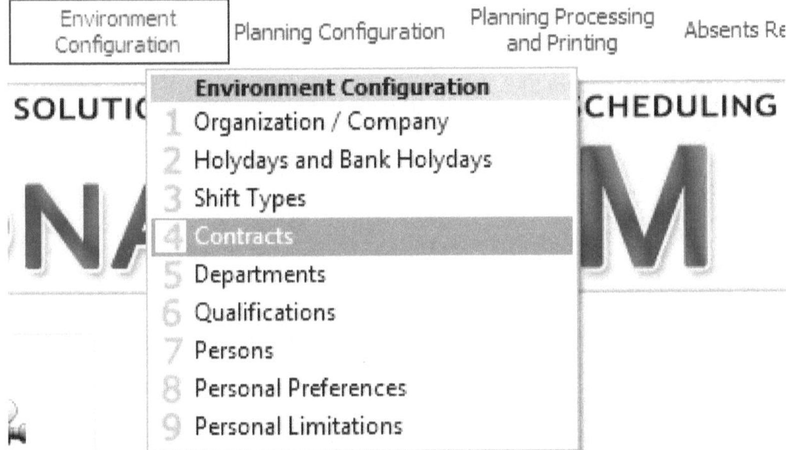

Contracts express the working conditions actually applied in our organization, and a contract must be configured for each kind of agreement actually used.

The contracts do not match the Collective Agreement Rules signed with trade unions and the like, but contain those obligations together with the working rules agreed in the individual situation with individual employees.

A contract must be configured for each existing employment relationship.

For example, if the cleaning staff were provided by an external supplier of workers on demand, we should set up a contract that expresses the conditions under which we employ the staff of this external supplier, although they are not our employees.

In "Smith Carpentry" we have four types of contracts: cleaning, part-time, full-time and full-time with overtime allowed.

The first contract is the contract which applies to some staff members that cover only two hours cleaning shifts; they work only twelve hours per week.

This means two hours per day, and twelve hours every seven days.

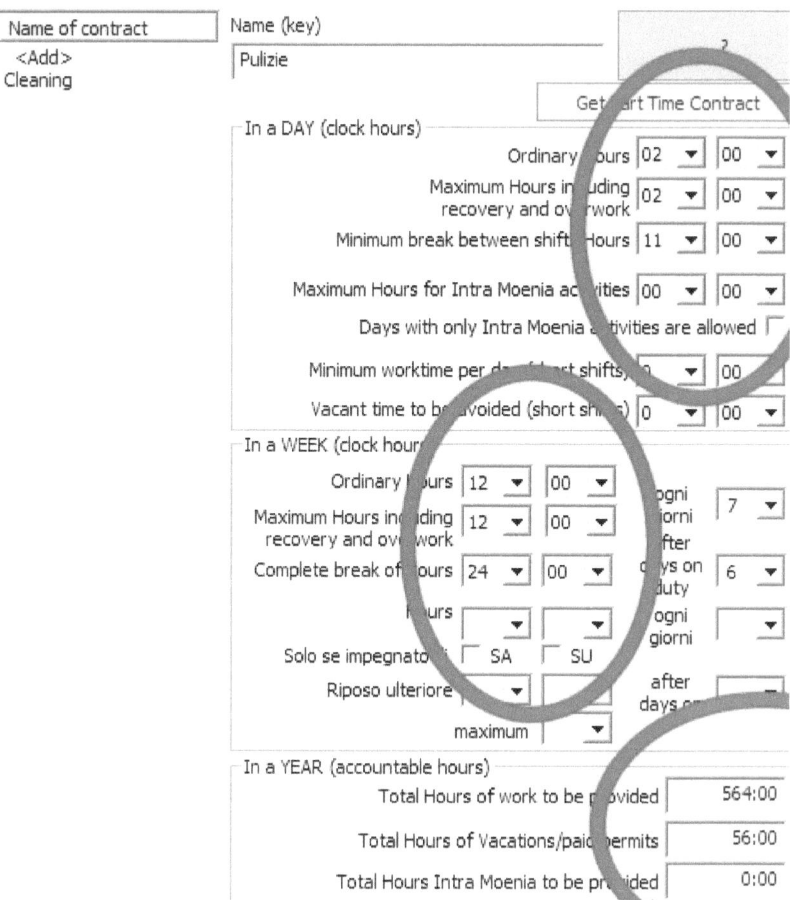

The second contract is the part-time contract, which allows a maximum of 8 hours per day (therefore no overtime) and 24 hours per week.

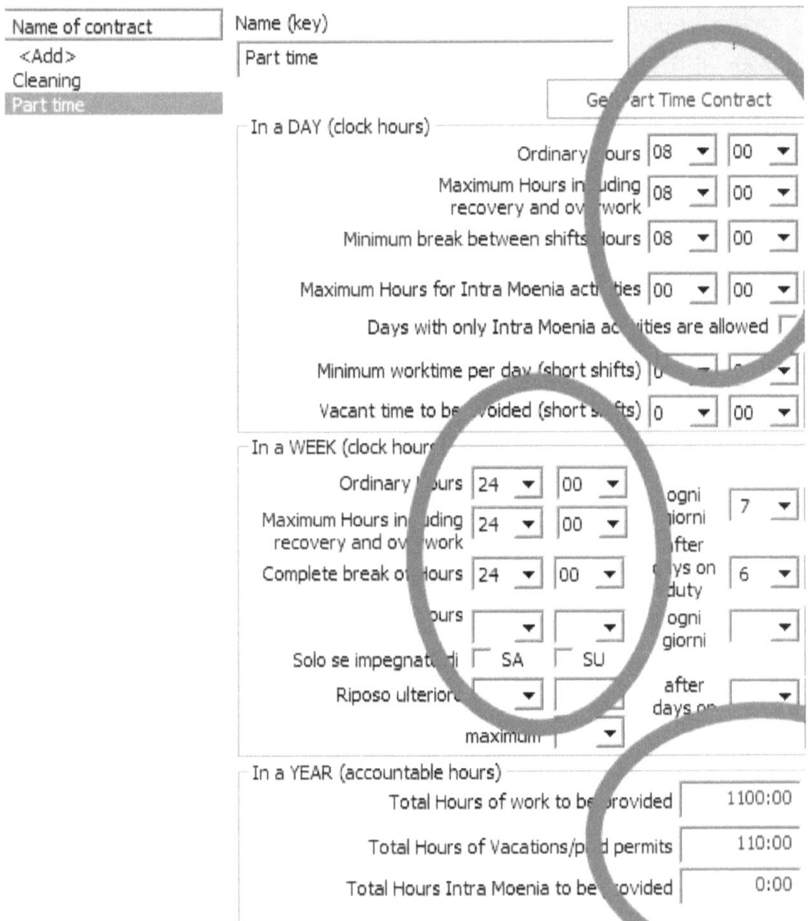

The third contract, full time, is applied to the majority of employees, and provides 40 hours per week without overtime.

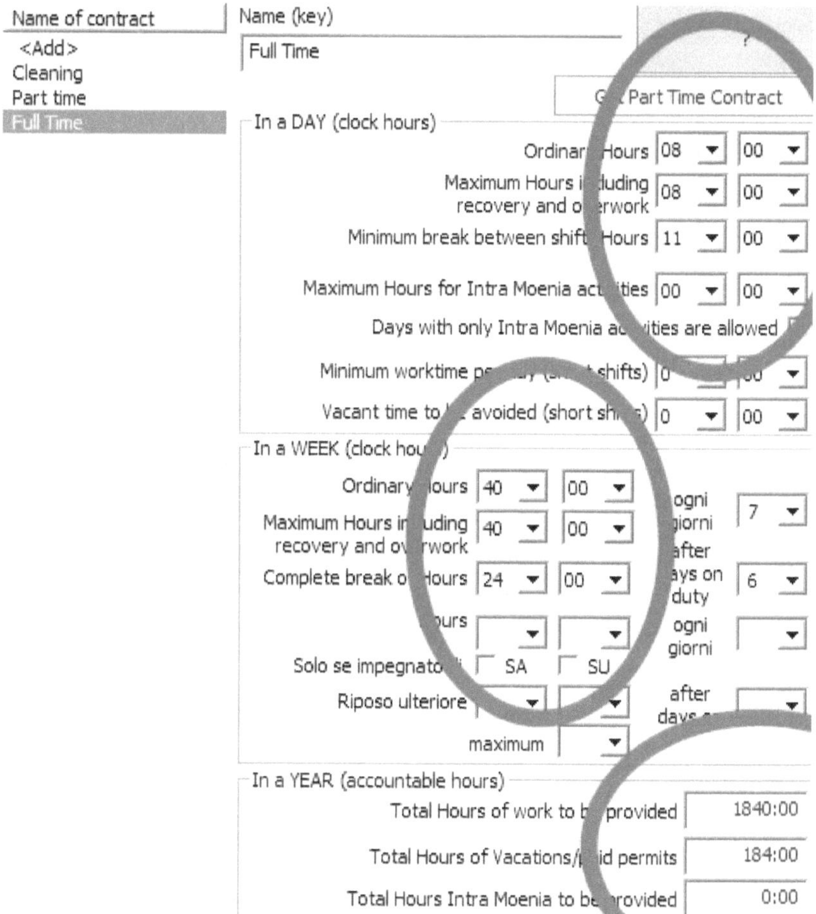

The fourth contract is applied to certain employees who can cover the cleaning shift when the Cleaners are absent or on leave. They can also work up to 48 hours a week instead of 40, with eight hours overtime, if is necessary to cover the staff requirements.

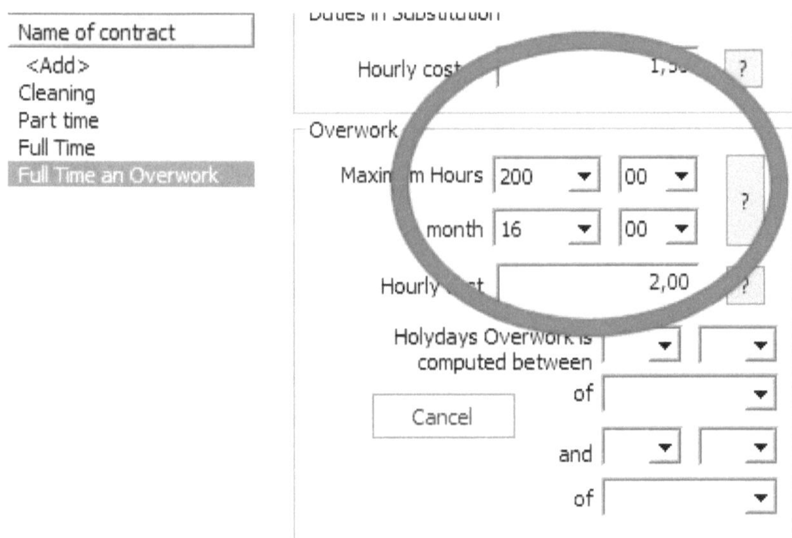

So in this contract, the standard work hours are 8 per day, but the maximum is 10 hours, because sometimes workers cover the cleaning shift in addition to the morning shift. In a week, the maximum is 48 hours.

To allow the overtime, you must configure a limit on a monthly and annual basis: in our case, the limit is 16 hours in the month and 200 in the year.

We will see how ZonaTEAM will try to minimize, and if possible to avoid, the use of overtime.

Departments

The next step is configuring the existing departments. In our case, the departments are only two, carpentry and painting.

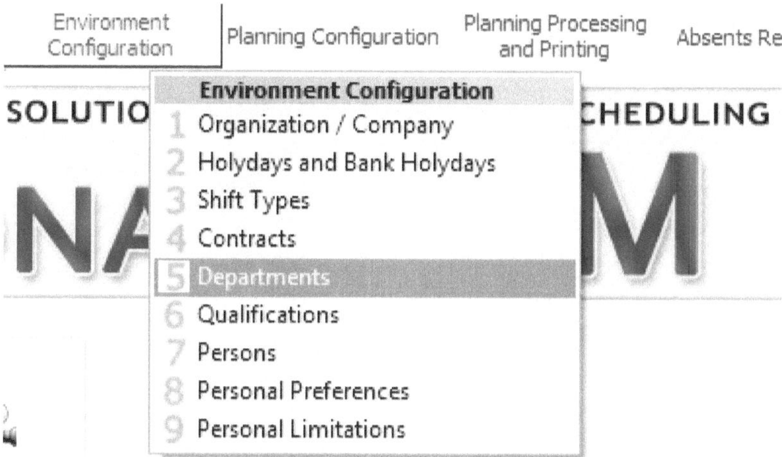

Warning: departments are the places where the work is done, and should not be confused with the qualifications, i.e. the kind of work performed; this is set up in the next step.

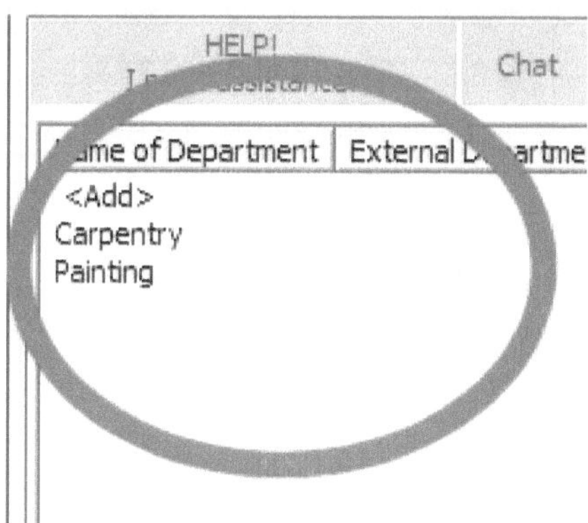

In the right panel we have some special data, which are useful in special situations; we will examine them only after having successfully completed a basic planning.

Qualifications

The next step is inserting the qualifications, i.e. the kinds of work performed by the employees.

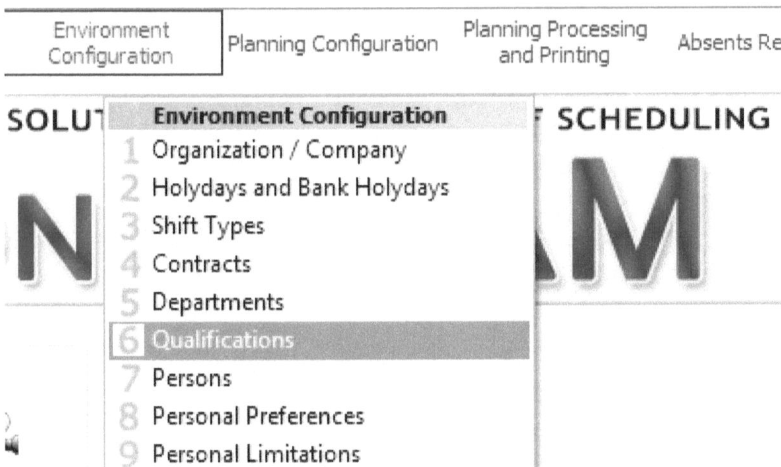

In our example, we have the following qualifications: Operative, Foreman and Cleaning Agent. All the three qualifications are required in both the carpentry and painting department.

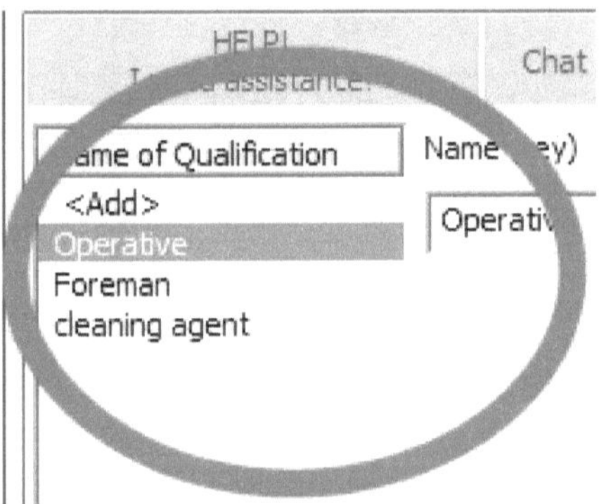

By setting up the configuration, you should take care not to multiply unnecessarily departments and qualifications, but create the fewest possible.

For example, in our case, since some members of staff are qualified to be the Foreman in the carpentry department and others in the painting department, the error that you could make would be to create the distinct qualifications of carpentry Foreman and painting Foreman. This redundancy would be useless, and would make the next steps in the configuration more difficult.

Staff members

The setup of staff members must be done carefully: for every person you need to specify the contract that applies, and then the qualifications to which the person is enabled.

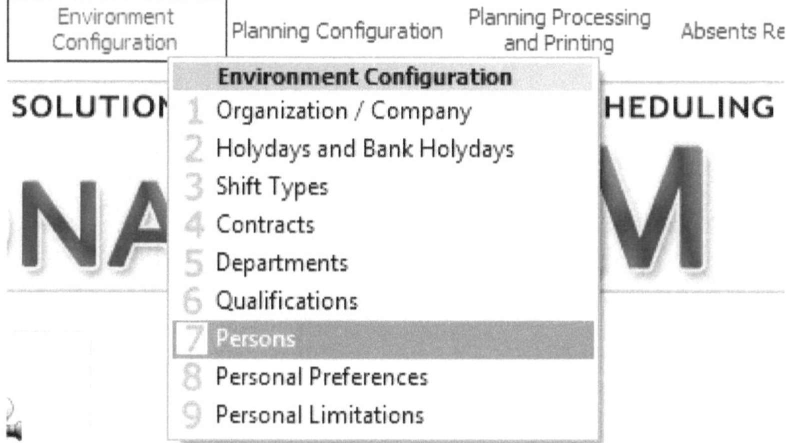

To work efficiently, you should start by inserting all the people together with what kind of contract they have, and then review the entire list and specify the qualifications allowed.

To work faster, you can use the "Copy properties" and "Paste properties" keys to assign the same allowed qualifications to more people.

Let's take a look at some examples from "Smith Carpentry".

Alexander has a full-time contract, and can only have Operative qualification in all departments. He cannot be a Foreman, and cannot take cleaning shifts.

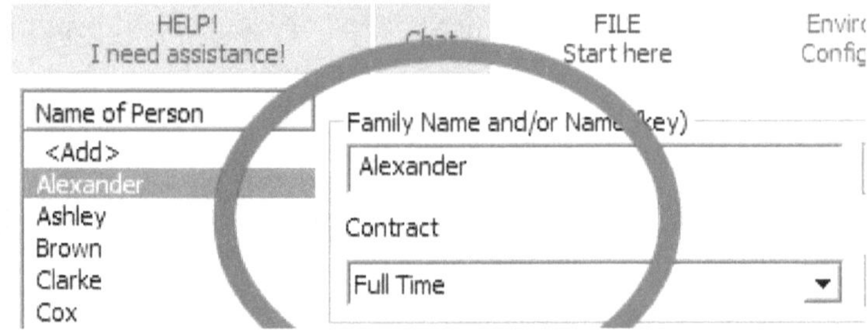

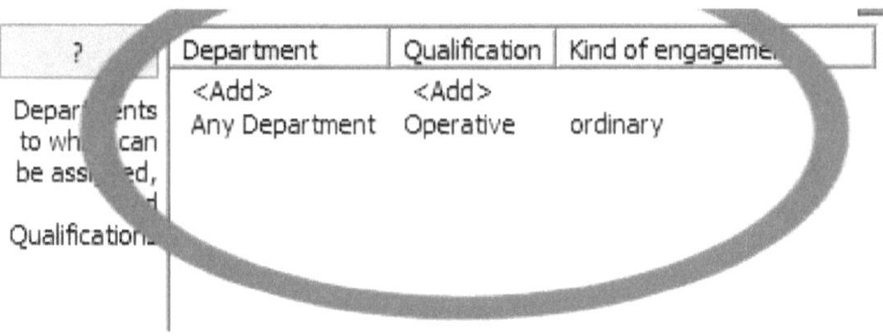

Mason has a part-time cleaning contract, and may only work as an Operative.

Cox has a full time contract that allows overtime, so he can cover some of his Operative colleagues shifts when needed, and a few cleaning shifts when the Cleaners are absent.

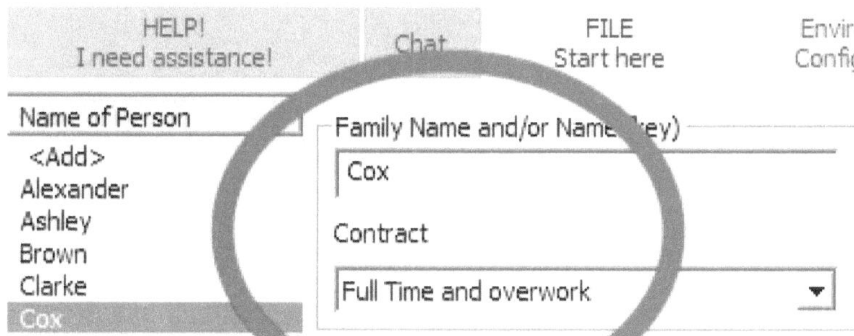

It's important to note that the status as Operative is ordinary, while the status of Housekeeping Attendant is configured as a replacement. This means that the automatic processing of planning will not assign him the qualification of Cleaner except when the Cleaners are insufficient to cover the scheduled work.

In the same way, employees authorized to cover the position of Foreman can cover the Operative status only as a replacement, i.e., when there are not enough employees to qualify as ordinary Operatives.

Smith can replace the Operatives if needed in any department, but his standard job is Foreman in the painting department. He cannot perform the job of Foreman in other departments, namely in carpentry.

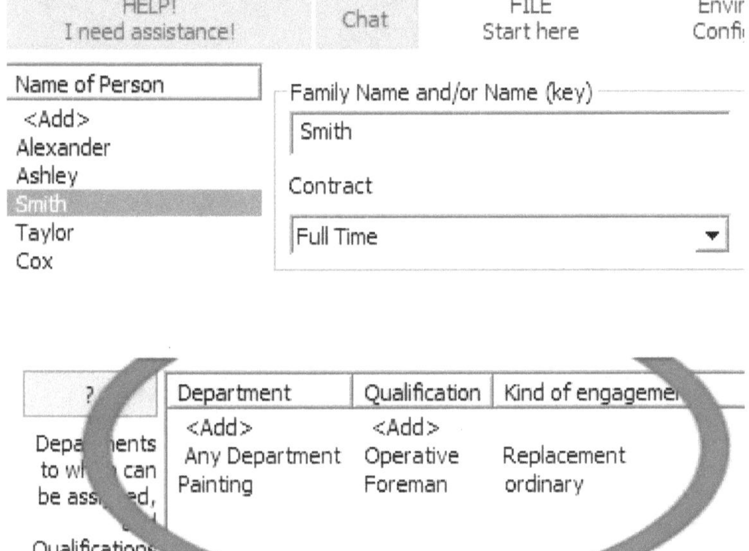

The employee Taylor is similar to Smith, but may perform the job of Foreman in any department.

Finally, Thomas can perform the job of Foreman in any department, but he cannot replace the Operatives, because when he is not engaged in work shifts he is available for management tasks not included in the schedule.

Personal preferences

Many personal preferences can also be configured. It's best not to use these fields the first time around: it is better to come back to these pages after having got the result of a simple rough draft.

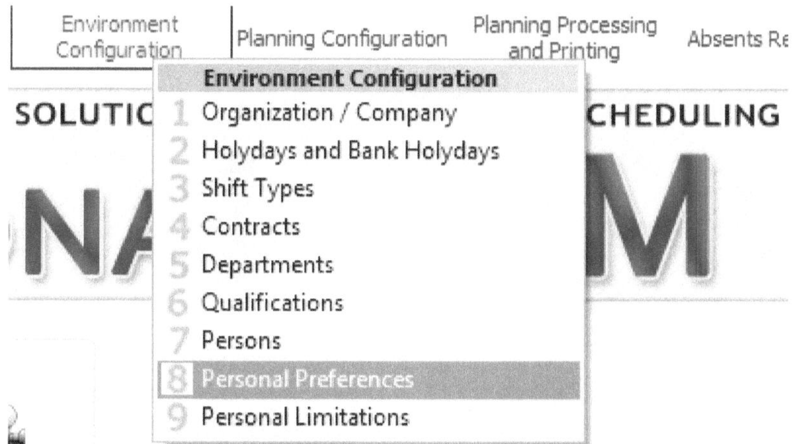

However, by way of example, we insert a preference for Jones, who cannot make more than 10% of his working time in night shifts for personal reasons.

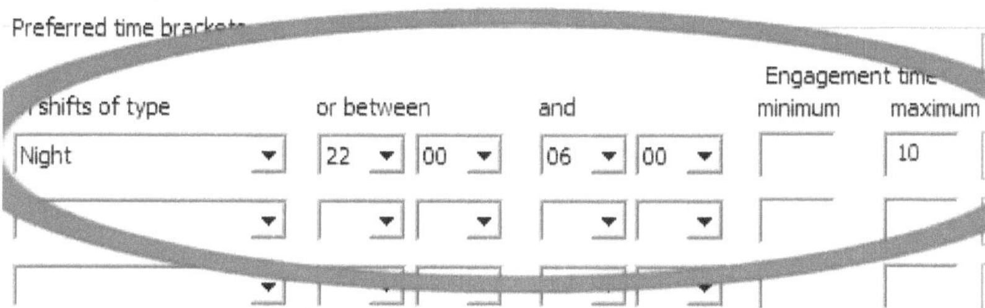

Personal limitations

Also the personal limitations will be considered only after you have completed a first configuration with no personal constraints.

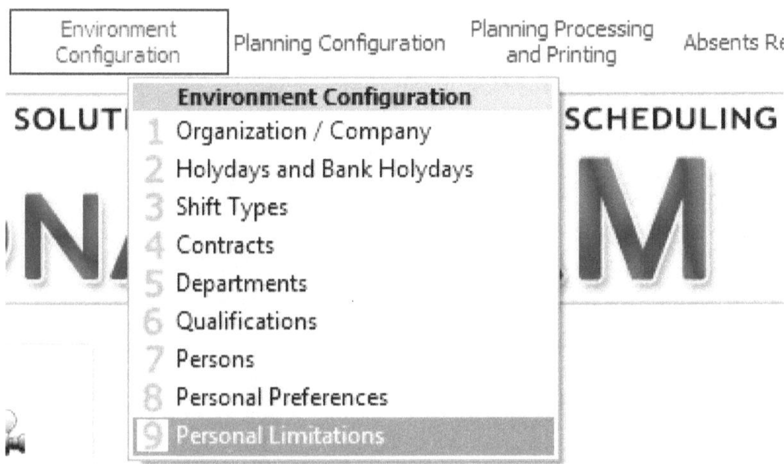

The personal limitations allow us to forbid certain departments or certain qualifications in given days or hours for a given person.

Personal preferences and limitations generally affect the time frames of getting the work done.

Mandatory Tutor

One of the personal limitations, however, is different: it is the constraint of the mandatory Tutor, which generally applies to apprentices or inexperienced employees.

In our example, Jackson may be engaged as an Operative in the carpentry department only if another Operative with the same qualification is present: obviously this Operative, which will be Jackson's instructor, should not have the obligation of having a Tutor.

In this example, Jackson may be committed in the painting department even without the presence of the Tutor.

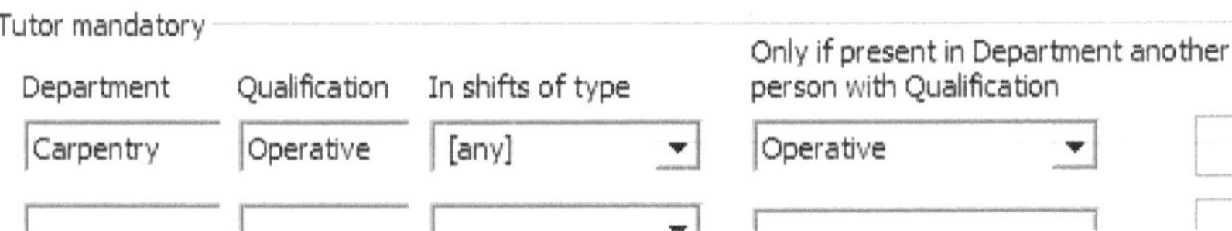

The Tutor constraint is used also when a person having a legal professional qualification degree is required in a given department. Employees that can work in that department but do not yet have the needed degree will be configured with mandatory Tutor.

Planning configuration

Now the configuration of the environment is ready, and we can go to setup the planning data.

At this point it is advisable to take advantage of the possibility of storing data on the cloud, keeping a copy of the work done so far. By doing so, you will be sure not to lose the work completed, and if necessary, you can retrieve it later.

The Cloud saving button is available on the main page.

Store Data on
Cloud and USB
Pen

Every time you reach a significant result you should store the configuration on the cloud, giving it a name that this will then remind us when and why we performed the backup.

Period to be planned

The first step is to set the time period to be planned.

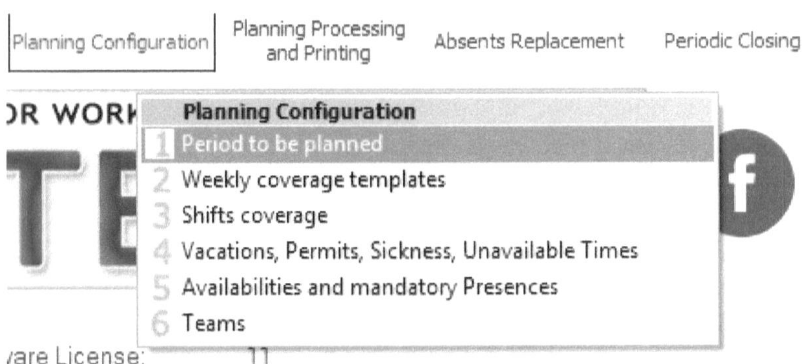

Initially schedule only one month, then you'll see whether it makes sense to plan for shorter periods (weeks) or longer- months at a time.

You should not plan long periods of time: the changes involved (holidays, dismissals, new hires) make such long periods unadvisable.

In our case, we plan between the 1st and 28th February.

There are cases where it is preferable not to plan from the first to the last day of the month, but from the first Monday of the month until the last Sunday, or until the first Sunday of the following month. This a practical choice that depends on the nature of your organization.

Weekly coverage templates

Next, we could configure the weekly coverage templates, but they are useful only in special cases and in a first test they should be neglected.

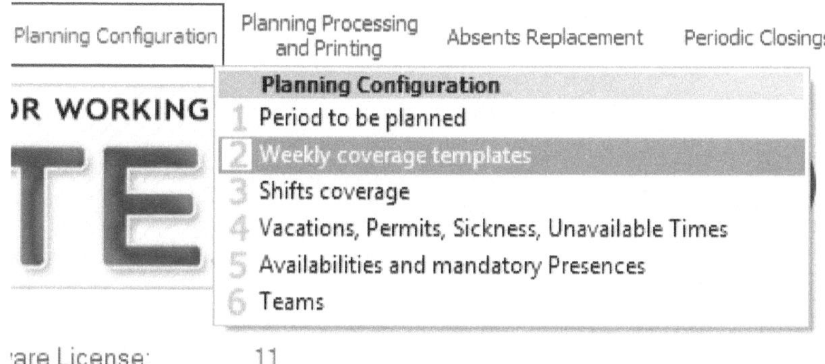

Let us briefly acknowledge this aspect, which could prove useful later.

The weekly coverage templates are useful in organizations that are based on different weekly patterns.

For example, the planning of a pharmacy could be based on the alternation between the ordinary weeks, in which the shop is open only during working days, and high duty weeks, in which the shop is open also on holidays and night hours. The coverage templates allow you to keep the information about the staff required and the shifts that must be covered in the two kinds of weeks, and then puts them quickly in monthly schedules.

Before using the templates of weekly coverage familiarize yourself with the configuration of the shift coverage, in the next step.

Later, if your planning is based on alternating weeks of different types, you will find it practical to use weekly coverage templates.

Shifts coverage

While the weekly templates are used only in special cases, the coverage of shifts must always be entered.

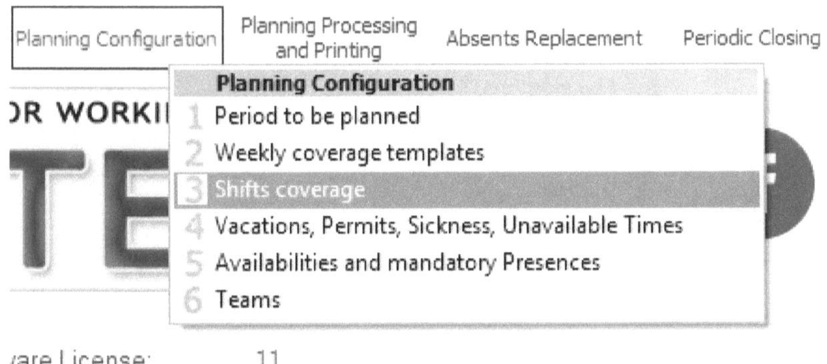

We must specify how many employees we need every day, in what kinds of shift, in which departments and with which qualifications. The planning of the "Smith Carpentry" requires sixteen elements of shift coverage.

Prog...	Days to be covered	Depart...	Qualification	Shift type	Staff
<Ad...					
1	MO-TU-WE-TH-FR	Carpen...	Operative	Morning (06:00-14:00)	3
2	MO-TU-WE-TH-FR	Painting	Operative	Morning (06:00-14:00)	3
3	MO-TU-WE-TH-FR	Carpen...	Operative	Afternoon (14:00-22:00)	3
4	MO-TU-WE-TH-FR	Painting	Operative	Afternoon (14:00-22:00)	3
5	MO-TU-WE-TH	Carpen...	Operative	Night (22:00-06:00)	2
6	MO-TU-WE-TH	Painting	Operative	Night (22:00-06:00)	2
7	MO-TU-WE-TH-FR-SA	Carpen...	Cleaning ...	Cleaning (14:00-16:00)	1
8	MO-TU-WE-TH-FR-SA	Painting	Cleaning ...	Cleaning (14:00-16:00)	1
9	MO-TU-WE-TH-FR-SA	Carpen...	Foreman	Morning (06:00-14:00)	1
10	MO-TU-WE-TH-FR-SA	Painting	Foreman	Morning (06:00-14:00)	1
11	MO-TU-WE-TH-FR	Carpen...	Foreman	Afternoon (14:00-22:00)	1
12	MO-TU-WE-TH-FR	Painting	Foreman	Afternoon (14:00-22:00)	1
13	MO-TU-WE-TH	Carpen...	Foreman	Night (22:00-06:00)	1
14	MO-TU-WE-TH	Painting	Foreman	Night (22:00-06:00)	1
15	-SA	Carpen...	Operative	Morning (06:00-14:00)	2
16	-SA	Painting	Operative	Morning (06:00-14:00)	2

Let's see some details.

From Monday to Friday, in the morning and in the afternoon, three employees are required with the qualification of Operative.

The night shift is expected only from Monday to Thursday, and requires two Operatives.

On Saturday there is only the morning shift, with two Operatives.

In all shifts, morning, afternoon and night, it is necessary to have a Foreman in addition to the Operatives. Therefore, these shifts are marked with priority.

The automatic processing of planning will take care to fill first the priority shifts, and then the other ones. So if the staff is not enough to cover everything, we will have some non-priority shifts with less people than required, but priority shifts will be entirely covered, unless the staff is widely understaffed so as not to be able to cover even the priority shifts.

Even the cleaning shifts have priority over the others.

Vacations and absences

After the coverage we can enter the leaves or absence that we know about in advance.

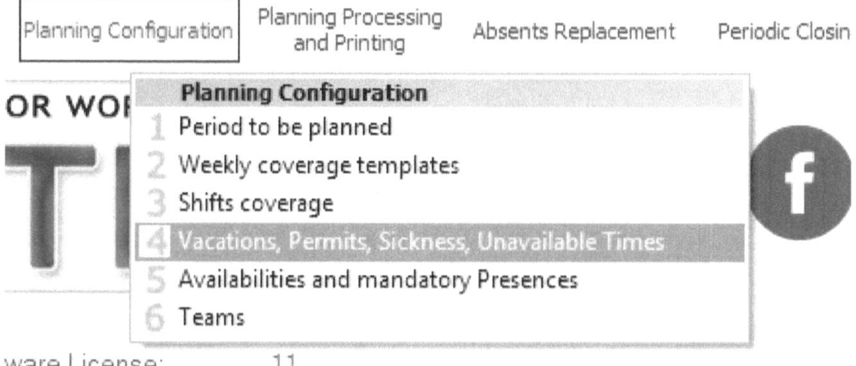

In our example, we insert five days of leave requested by Roberts, who is a Cleaner. Since every day we have a cleaning shift (with priority) in each department, and since the people having the qualification of Cleaning Agent as ordinary task are just two, we will see that some employees whose standard job is Operative will cover the cleaning shifts in replacement, in order to fill the gap in Roberts scheduled days off.

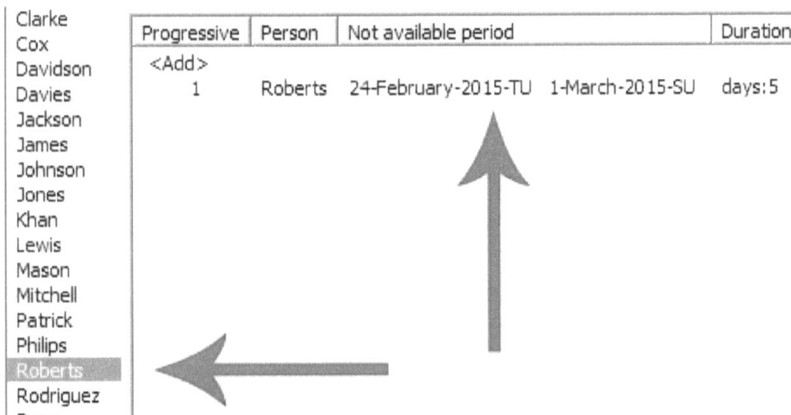

One detail: when you enter a leave or permit a period of illness, be careful to enter the reason of the absence.

Absences have different value in relation to the distribution of the workload on annual basis.

We shall come back later to this point.

Processing of planning

Now it is time to go to the processing of planning.

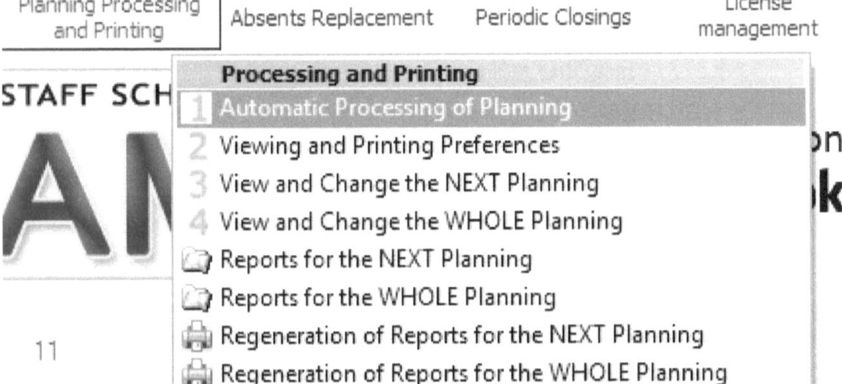

Because until now we have not assigned any shifts, when we enter the planning panel a total shortfall of staff is reported.

Initially, ZonaTEAM will calculate how many hours of work will be needed to meet the planed coverage, and in our case this makes a total of 3,616 hours of work, distributed in different departments and qualifications.

To get the planning we must perform the available tasks in the order suggested.

First, we test the feasibility of planning, which only serves to reveal any inconsistencies in the configuration, and to verify the absence of contradictory constraints.

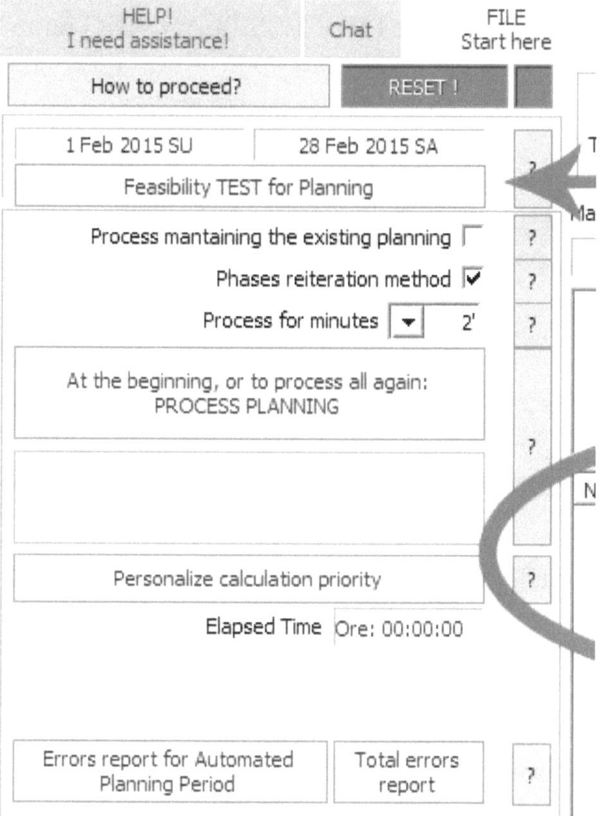

After a few moments, a message warns that the plan is feasible, and there are no blocking errors.

When you test your setup, if the feasibility test persists a long time without end, stop it with the STOP key and consult assistance. There is surely a mismatch inside the configuration that you find hard to identify, and which will be rather easy to be recognized by the assistance.

In order to get a first result quickly, we calculate the schedule using the phase reiteration method, for one or two minutes.

Processing will last a few more than the scheduled time.

We can configure the alarm sound (tam tam) that will attract our attention at the end of processing.

Launch processing with the **PROCESS PLANNING** button and let processing go on.

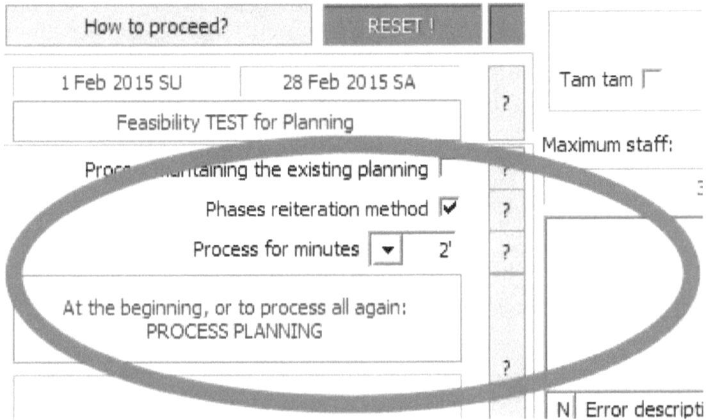

While processing, the upper window shows the progress achieved gradually. The central window shows the problems that hinder the finding of an optimal solution, but this information does not particularly interest us.

Having more experience using ZonaTEAM, you will learn to "read" these messages and to obtain information about your planning and the bottlenecks that slow the retrieval of the best results, but it is more likely that such things will never interest you. You can get excellent results without going into this technical detail: if you have doubts about optimization, please consult assistance.

While processing the STOP button is visible, and if necessary you can use it to stop processing.

After processing is complete, a few minutes later, we are notified of two things.

Some employees have been used for tasks in replacement or in overtime, which causes an additional costs that could be reduced or even brought to zero by a more prolonged processing.

Error description	Person	Contract	Quantity
Reduction to minimum of cost for Substitutions	Cox	Full Time and overwork	15:00
Reduction to minimum of cost for overwork	Cox	Full Time and overwork	16:00
Reduction to minimum of cost for Substitutions	Davies	Full Time and overwork	3:00
Reduction to minimum of cost for overwork	Davies	Full Time and overwork	4:00
Reduction to minimum of cost for Substitutions	Rose	Part Time	24:00
Reduction to minimum of cost for Substitutions	Smith	Full Time	12:00
Reduction to minimum of cost for Substitutions	Williams	Full Time	24:00
Staff Hours required for Department / Qualification	Carpentry-Op...		72:00
Staff Hours required for Department / Qualification	Carpentry-For...		16:00
Staff Hours required for Department / Qualification	Painting-Opera...		72:00

In addition, we have a deficit of staff of 258 hours: that is, shifts for 258 hours, 4. 5% of the total amount to be allocated, were not assigned.

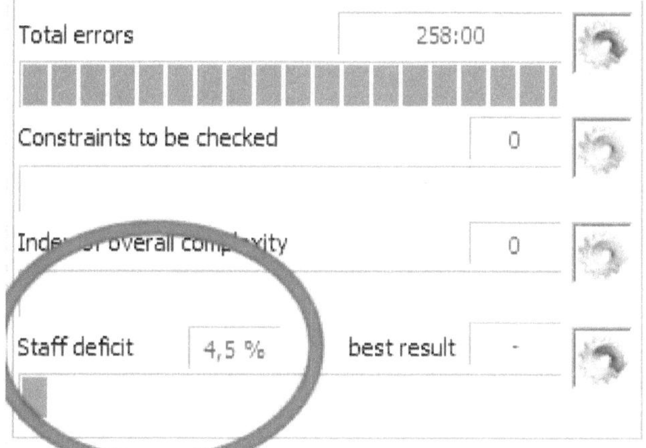

Also this deficit could be reduced or zeroed by longer processing.

Therefore we should process again and for a longer time.

But first let's see the result of the planning done. Let us go to see the next Planning.

Viewing the processed planning

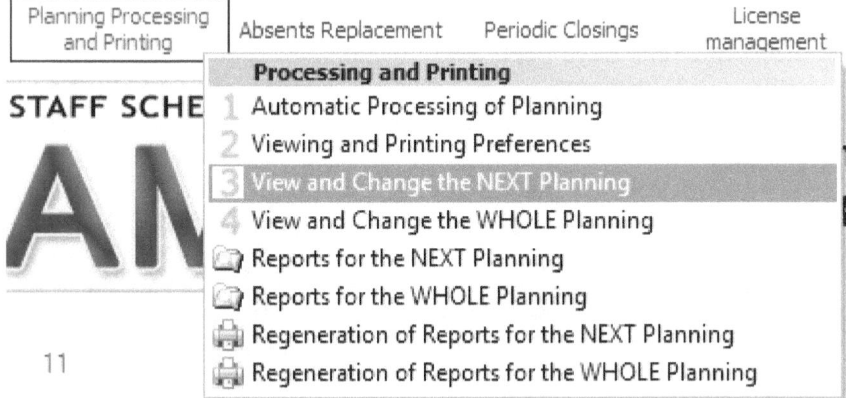

Some shifts, mainly those at night, have not been assigned.

The shifts that are not assigned are displayed first, in a different color.

Person	Department	Qualification	mo 2 2	tu 3 2 15	we 4 2 15	th 5 2 15
(not assigned)	Carpentry	Operative		A		
(not assigned)	Painting	Operative			N	
(not assigned)	Carpentry	Foreman				
Alexander	Painting	Operative	A	A		
Alexander	Carpentry	Operative			A	
Ashley	Carpentry	Operative	A	A	A	
Ashley	Painting	Operative				A
Brown	Carpentry	Operative	N			
Brown	Painting	Operative			N	N
Clarke	Carpentry	Operative	M			M
Clarke	Painting	Operative			M	
Cox	Painting	Operative	N			

You might try to assign unassigned shifts by hand selecting them, but you would realize immediately that this is not easy:

all attempts would violate a constraint, mainly because the people would work 16 hours a day. This would be shown in the error panel.

The panel would report errors in red.

The only way to complete the staff without violating constraints is to process for a longer time, letting ZonaTEAM work until a better result is found.

So let's go back to processing, and select a total of 20 minutes of processing.

The reiteration phases method allows for a more accurate result. All phases are performed in sequence repeatedly, first for a short time, then more slowly until the maximum time configured is reached.

Let us now process again and wait.

Shortly after passing the twenty minutes required for processing, the processing stops without any residual deficit of staff.

The shifts were fully assigned.

A few hours remain and can be used in replacements or with overtime.

Let's go view the result, and ask ourselves why there is use of tasks in replacement or overtime.

Employees Cox and Davies have been used for the shift of cleaning, Cox four times and Davies once, as is shown in the error panel. But we know that one of the Cleaners is on leave from 24th February onwards: so this replacement cannot be avoided.

Some shifts are assigned to foremen in replacement, when theoretically they could be assigned to the Operatives as an ordinary task. This depends on the staff we have available: all the hours per month due are assigned, but the Operatives are not enough to cover all their shifts, and then the foremen are engaged in replacement.

You can try to further reduce these hours of overtime or replacements by repeating the processing for another twenty minutes. If the result is the same, this means that the use of those hours of replacement or overtime cannot be avoided.

Tip: When you get a good result, to see if there is an even better result process again for twice as long as the previous time. If the result is identical to the previous one, it means that there is no arrangement of shifts better than the one found.

Detailed features

Now let's see some aspects in detail.

First, let's see how ZonaTEAM manages the accounting of time worked and of leaves enjoyed and to be enjoyed.

Work hours and vacation accounting

In every contract you must enter the total hours of work to be paid in the calendar year, and the total hours of leave.

For example, we have:

40 hours for 52 weeks = 2,080 hours.

Holidays & Permits: 30 days in all, then 8 hours for 30 days = 240 hours.

Hours to be paid = 2,080 - 240 = 1,840.

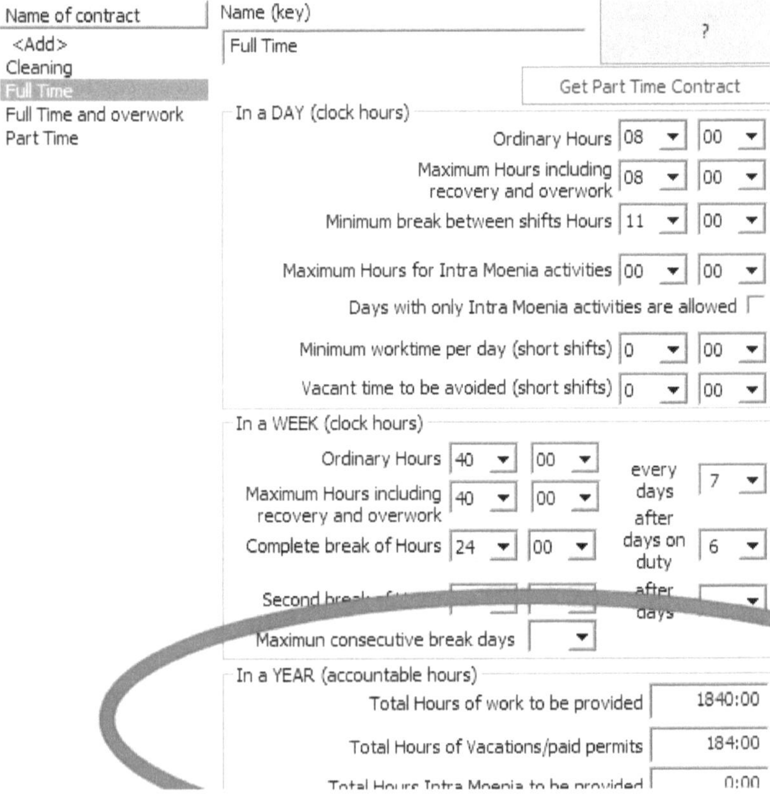

Enter this information carefully in order to best forecast your staffing needs using all the staff 100 % of the hours needed and without overtime.

Since ZonaTEAM has the goal to equally distribute the same percentage of work + holidays hours, it is important that these numbers correspond approximately to the total number of hours provided by employment contracts, but it is not necessary to be exact.

Instead, it is important that the annual number of work hours for part-time contracts be strictly proportional to the number of hours of corresponding full-time contracts.

For example, if we have employees at 40 hours per week and other employees at 20 hours per week, if we set up for the first ones 2,000 hours of work and 200 leave, and for the second ones 1,000 hours of work and 100 leave, ZonaTEAM will share the workload in the right way, recovering month after month any excess or deficit of paid work in the previous months.

If the annual number of hours of different contracts is not proportionate to the weekly amount, we will not have a correct distribution of the workload.

For consultants, substitutes, contractors etc. that are called into service only when the permanent staff is not sufficient, the annual work amount should be set roughly to a small amount. For external people called on demand to cover absences of our staff, for example, the staff provided by an external supplier of workers on demand, it is convenient to specify a very low number of hours, for example 10 or 100 hours per year: this limit is unlikely to be met, but it will help to minimize the use of external staff.

To obtain well proportioned values in part-time contracts, once the full-time contract is defined, a part-time contract can be derived using appropriate button, which opens a window in which you are requested the name of the new contract for part time to be configured automatically and the percentage of the part-time.

For each staff member the goal of working hours and holidays gradually achieved during the current year is highlighted.

In the planning that we have just developed, employees qualified as Operatives have all provided about 152 hours of work during the month of February and are all brought to about 97.9 % of the target.

In the planning viewing panel the target achieved is also highlighted.

Alexander has reached 107.7 % of his target.

Johnson has also reached 96. 4% of his goal, and February 3rd he might work the afternoon shift without violating constraints.

Johnson, who has reached 97,9% of his goal, asked to be free in the Afternoon of February 3rd.

We select the afternoon shift for Johnson on February 3rd and we give it to Jackson. To do this, we simply select the shift to move, and assign it to another person using the "Engage" button.

Once that's done, the panel of errors does not show anything, so the movement of the shift did not violate any constraint.

The bottom panel of errors gives us evidence of the task performed, which could be cancelled by pressing the "one step back" button.

Instead, we accept the operation performed. Consequently, the Johnson goes from 152 to 144 hours worked in the year since January 1, and switches to 92.8 % of total Work + Holiday consumed.

Instead Jackson goes to 152 hours and 102.0% of the target.

Theoretically, we could look for an eight-hour shift in the rest of February planning and move it from Jackson to Johnson

in order to balance the account of both employees.

But it is not necessary: when processing the next month, ZonaTEAM will automatically put the accounts in balance.

During the year, the holidays will be enjoyed by all employees, and gradually we will keep an eye on the trend of the goal achieved by each of them, and we will control that at the end of the year all will indicate the same percentage of Job + Holidays, around the 100%.

If this does not happen, it means that some employees did not enjoy all the holidays entitled by contract, and others enjoyed more: we can carry the accounts over the next year and balance the accounts during the next years.

As a result of all this, in order to have an exact management of working time and holidays, it is important to enter thoroughly all the leave periods enjoyed.

This can be done in two ways.

If the vacation period is scheduled before the processing of planning, we insert the holidays provided for in the schedule configuration.

We have already seen this case for the employee Roberts, who had taken some days off in the last week of February.

If the holidays are required after planning has been processed, it is during the scheduled time, the days of leave shall be specified in the planning viewing panel.

In our example, Ashley asked for a leave on February 3rd. So we removed eight hours of work for Ashley, decreasing the overall goal of Job + Holidays from 96.7 % to 92.8%.

But suppose you want to account the full eight hours as vacation, and you want them to increase the vacation amount .

To do this, we must select the day for February 3rd Johnson, and use the "Add a Vacation or Permit" button.

Once this is done, Ashley's vacation account indicates eight hours taken, and the overall goal returns to 102. 0 %. Ashley no longer needs to provide those eight hours of recovery, but he has one less day of vacation.

Priority of processing phases

The second detailed feature of planning we want to mention in this chapter is the priority of the optimizations in the processing of the schedule.

The process of planning first assigns shifts to people without violating any mandatory condition expressed by contracts and any constraint imposed by the planned holidays and absences, by personal preferences and by availability and mandatory presence.

Once this is done, several other goals remain: to fill the workforce to the maximum, to minimize the use of overtime and replacements, to balance with the utmost fairness Work + Holidays for each employee, and other goals as equitable distribution of Sundays and organization of the work shifts as homogeneous as possible, thereby minimizing alternating mornings and afternoons.

For each of these goals, the software calculates the best possible result proceeding in phases. Each phase corresponds to a goal.

The first step is always the filling of staff.

The software tries to fill 100% of the shifts that have been configured.

The next phases are processed in a default sequence that is good in most cases: the most important goal to be achieved is that of reducing, and if possible, zeroing, overtime and replacements, then following the equitable distribution of Work + Holidays, while the less important phase is the organization of work in teams.

Each phase ends automatically, and moves to the next, when its goal is achieved at 100 % or if there is no goal to reach, because nothing is configured. Otherwise the phases terminate automatically after a certain time.

The sequence of the phases can be customized if the default sequence does not match your needs.

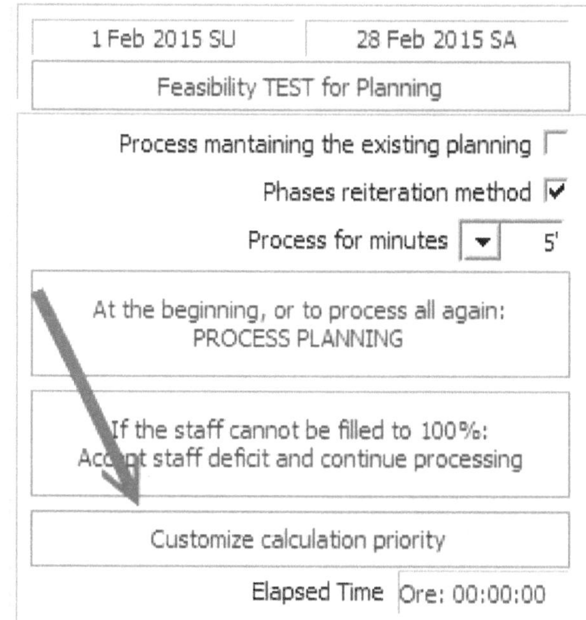

The button " Customize the calculation priority " allows us to change the priority of the phases, but the filling of shifts is always first phase.

For example, in many organizations the equitable distribution of work and leave is considered more important than the reduction of overtime and replacements.

If you want to set up your own priority, you have to select the phase of processing "equitable distribution of Work +Vacation" and move it up, increasing its priority, using the "Move up" button.

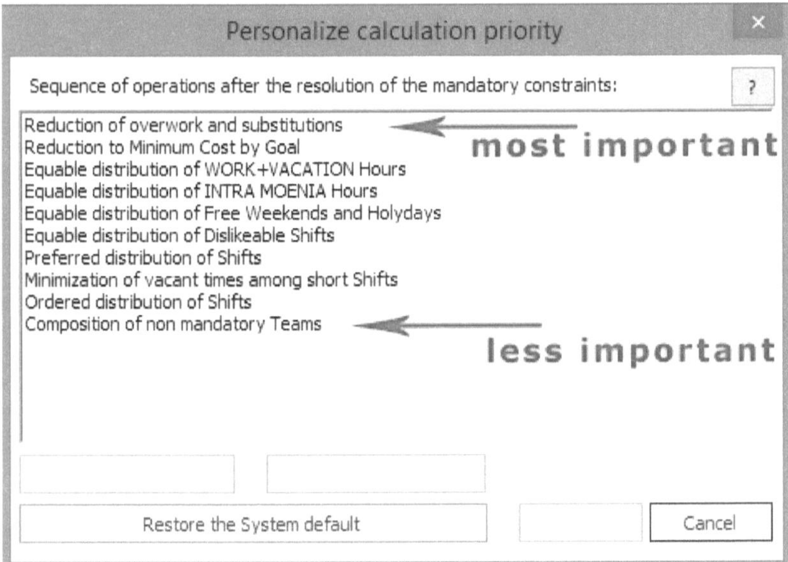

Changing the priority of the optimization phases significantly changes the result of the processing.

To focus on your needs in this regard, consult assistance.

Overall temporal organization of planning

The third detail which we wish to mention concerns the overall temporal organization of planning.

Suppose we start working on the first day of January of a given year and to plan the schedule from January 1st to 31st.

The first processed planning has the name "next planning", and includes the month of January.

Suppose now, about January 20th, we want to begin planning for February. To do this, we change the planning period setting it from February 1st until February 28th, and then we start the new plan. The new February data is linked to that of January, but does not modify it.

At this point, after processing, we have two schedules: one called "next ", which now includes the month of February, and one called "whole" which includes both January and February.

At any moment we can display and print the next planning and the whole planning.

The "next" Planning is the current one and refers to the immediate future.

The "whole" planning includes the whole available data, past and present, and theoretically could also be extended over several years.

Account Closings

Old information that accumulates causes problems.

Therefore, during each year, it is advisable to perform an *inter-annual closing* from time to time.

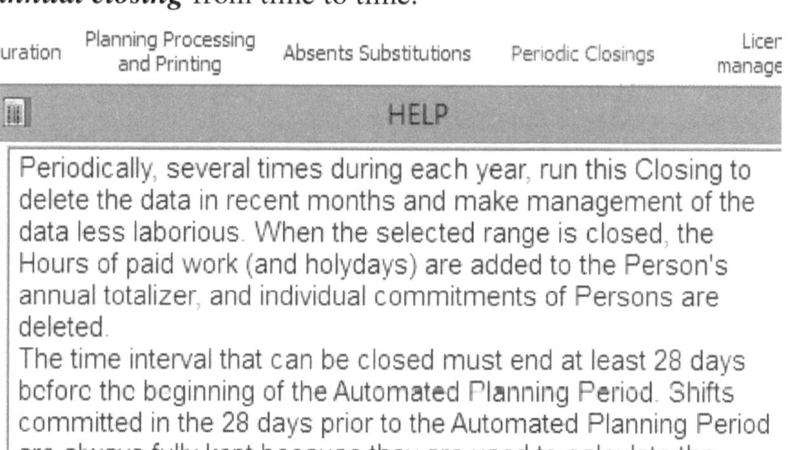

When the inter-annual closing is performed, the individual shifts assigned in the past planning are erased, but their values of Work and Vacation hours are added to the global counters of each staff member.

The "next" planning remains unchanged.

You should close the past planning retaining the detailed data of the last two or three months; in any case the software will keep the full data of the last four weeks before the next planning.

Before closing, read the instructions, and make a backup on Cloud: sometimes it may be useful to restore and consult the old detailed data.

During the month of January or February of each new year, it is advisable to proceed with the closure of the previous year.

nning Configuration	Planning Processing and Printing	Absents Substitutions	Periodic Closings

⠿	HELP

Early in every year (generally in one of the first days of January), run the Closing of the previous year. The total amount of worked hours (and holydays) in the current year is deleted and summed to the previous years total. In this way the calculation of due hours of work and holyday is reset for the new year.
Note: the start date of a year relevant for the calculation of working Hours to be granted is not necessarily January 1 - it could be, for example, the first Monday of the year, or the last Monday of the previous year. It depends on how you want to calculate the progressive total of worked Hours of the year, which could be calculated from January 1 to December 31, for example, or for 52 weeks, from first Monday of the old year until the first Sunday of the new year, or other such criteria.

Again read the instructions carefully, and make a backup on Cloud before proceeding.

Back cover

Scheduling staff shifts is a difficult task. In organizations that work on Sundays, and/or on public holidays, and/or during night hours, scheduling shifts accurately and efficiently is a time consuming job, and it also exposes employers to the risk of excessive overtime costs and poor distribution of workload among employees.

In order to be efficient, anyone who has the task of planning the activities of an organization must learn to perform two activities that are interconnected but distinct: first, he must learn to represent the data specific to his organization's problem in an organized manner, ideally resolving the matter manually, with pen and paper; then, he must learn to use a software dedicated to the problem of shift scheduling.

This book teaches how to address the problem of allocating tasks systematically, and also teaches how to use a dedicated software program to achieve this purpose without wasting time with repetitive tasks in search of the best organizational solution, operations that can be performed by a computer.

Thus, in this book we will first discuss the data analysis of the problem that needs to be addressed before making use of any software tool. We will then proceed by giving examples and referring to one of the most efficient and cheap software solutions available on the market: ZonaTEAM, produced by Zonabit Sistemi.

Attentive readers of this book will become experts in planning, and will acquire the ability to plan with full and rational use of available human resources, saving in overtime costs, all the while providing fair treatment of employees.

Isabella Longobardi

Isabella Longobardi was born in Palermo in 1960, and lives in Rome, where she is a computer science teacher and consultant. Expert in solving organization and management optimization problems, she cooperated in the design of algorithms for the automatic scheduling of school timetables and shifts rosters. She is also web master and technical manager of the publisher *il glifo*, for which she developed many software tools for optimal generation of electronic books.